DADDY

T0329444

Colin Diyen

Langaa Research & Publishing CIG
Mankon, Bamenda

Publisher:
Langaa RPCIG
Langaa Research & Publishing Common Initiative Group
P.O. Box 902 Mankon
Bamenda
North West Region
Cameroon
Langaagrp@gmail.com
www.langaa-rpcig.net

Distributed in and outside N. America by African Books Collective
orders@africanbookscollective.com
www.africanbookcollective.com

ISBN: 9956-791-49-0

© Colin Diyen 2013

Dedication

This book is dedicated to the following old men, all of blessed memory, who have had a great impact in my life: HRH Ngam John Sabinla; Bah Maya Azah, Leo Nkwain Mbang, Bartholomeo Ndim Njong and Isidore Irvine Diyen.

1

My father was one of those old chaps who lived fast, although he didn't die young. He was a jovial, happy fellow, always fun to be with and quite easy going. My wife Mawumi appreciated him immensely and visited him as often as she could. My mother always declared that God had given her a pearl in that old man, and they both made a couple that anyone would admire. The couple was known as Mr. and Mrs. Ngongnuwi.

Mr. Ngongnuwi for his part loved me very much, but I suspected that he loved his daughter in-law even more. He would flatter Mawumi like a French lover wooing a very soft and pretty lady, and would shower her with gifts and praises whenever possible. Dad made regular visits to my home or office, and these visits made my day worth living. Yes, we had lots of fun together.

Our best times were when we were having a drink together. In their home, my mother often frowned at his attempts to drink alcohol, although he generally pleaded and had his way. But then, drinking alone was not quite enjoyable. In the presence of Mawumi, my old man's drinking was also kind of controlled. If he wanted to drink freely and enjoy his booze completely, he normally showed up at my office and both of us would sneak off to some jolly corner where he could imbibe the stuff undisturbed by uncompromising females.

At times, if we decided on cognac or some hard stuff, we simply hit the bottle in my office. Being a man of the bottle, too, I was convinced that the women were exaggerating a bit about the effect of alcohol on dad's health. He was still very athletic and fit, and quite robust when it came to the booze. He did not look at all like some of those frail, ancients. Again, I had never seen my father roaring drunk and staggering. We knew our limits

One day in the afternoon as dad came visiting as usual, I told him about a new place I had discovered. Apart from booze, there was wonderful roasted beef and pork. Unlike most of his peers, my dad did not suffer from gout, high blood pressure or diabetes. When we were together just two of us, he could eat anything that was forbidden to old men. Medically, he was not barred from any food or spice and was free to take sugar, salt, and any cooking fat or oil. His only limitations in the consumption of certain delicacies came from my mother and Mawumi, who were both of the opinion that indulging in too much beef and cholesterol-jammed food could eventually provoke some of those ailments that inflicted most old men. I rather thought that if at his age he was still free from those ailments and quite fit, then he should be allowed to enjoy his alcohol and excess protein. My father loved beef and pork even better than chicken, which the women often imposed on him.

As soon as dad heard about the new joint, he urged me to take him there.

"It is not far from here," I said, "so we can simply stroll over."

"I hope you don't want to punish an old man with too much exercise," Dad said.

"I want you to get really thirsty so that the beer will flow right through your veins," I said.

"And what happens to the grilled meat?" the old man asked, laughing. "Anyway, I'd like to stroll a bit."

About twenty five meters away from my office, we came to an undertaker's shop and my father stopped to admire some coffins.

"Now let's look at these." he said, moving closer to thoroughly examine the coffins. "This is quite beautiful," he said, pointing at one of them. "It is wonderful."

I gave no response. Coffins scared me and it felt eerie standing there admiring containers for dead bodies.

"You are not saying anything?" Dad asked "Only a dumb fellow would stand in front of such a beauty and remain mute. This is a masterpiece."

"I wonder whether I will ever be able to admire or appreciate coffins," I said.

"In that case," Dad said, "you will never be able to choose a good one for me when I die, and I should rather make my choice now. I would like to be buried in this very coffin that I am showing you."

"But, dad," I protested "you can't be talking of a coffin now while you still have a long time to live."

"Who wants to continue living when he has discovered a beautiful thing like that coffin in which he could sleep forever?" dad said. "I wish I could die now."

I was horrified. For such a lively old man to start talking about death is such a scary thing.

"Dad," I said, "you don't have to die because you have seen a coffin that you like. Many other beautiful coffins will be made and when you finally die you will have a wide choice."

"And who will make that choice for me?" he asked. "You who know nothing about good coffins? Or shall it be that my corpse will stroll to the undertaker's and use my expertise to choose a good one?"

3

I realized that he was right. Dead men don't make choices on anything.

"If you insist on this one," I said, "we shall buy a similar one and bury you in it, although I am sure that it will be quite a number of decades from now."

"That is just the point." Dad said. "If I take long to die, you might have forgotten about this coffin and, even if you do remember, it might no longer be there to buy."

"Dad," I said, "you should forget about coffins for now and concentrate on things that are useful to the body and keep you going."

"Like what?" he asked.

"Like our usual booze," I said. "That is what you should be thinking about now, not coffins."

"You know what son?" the old chap said. "I don't want to take chances and I don't quite trust you in these things. I will buy this coffin and keep it till I die. Then I will die satisfied that I will be buried in a beautiful coffin."

I was horrified at that statement.

"That will be a terrible thing to do Dad." I said "It will keep reminding you about death."

"And I will be happy about that," he said, "for it will keep reminding me that there is a full guarantee that I will be buried in a choice coffin."

Dad went in, talked with the salesman, and paid for the coffin. I was left with the task of conveying it to his house and keeping it in a safe place. Since we still had our boozing spree ahead of us, I arranged to collect it the next day.

When we had finally sat down and ordered our beer and grilled meat, I turned to my father.

"Father, this coffin thing," I said

"What coffin thing?" he asked, interrupting me.

"I mean this determination to own a coffin while you are still alive and certainly have a long way to go," I said "Did you take it from your father?"

"What do you mean?" he asked.

"It is quite strange that you are not even ill, yet you start worrying about a coffin and insist on a coffin of your choice. Did my grandfather make his own choice of coffin before he died?" I asked.

"No," Dad replied. "You realize that it was simply a matter of luck that brought me across this most appropriate coffin and I thus had the opportunity to make a good choice."

"So you may never have been bothered about a coffin if you had not come across this one?" I asked.

"Actually," dad said, "I was extremely fortunate to have stumbled across a coffin I like while still conscious enough to make the choice. Many people are not that lucky. Your grandfather was not that lucky. Besides, such beautiful coffins were not yet available when my father lived so I had to choose for him when he died. I only hope my choice was appropriate and close to what he would have loved to be buried in."

"So you don't want to give me the opportunity to choose a coffin for you?" I asked.

"You have good tastes in other things, son, but not in coffins, I am certain. I am particular about my choice of coffin because it will be my bed forever. It has to be quite appropriate."

I gave up. If I could, I would have invited the pirate who declared that "dead man don't bite" to come and explain to my dad that dead men are really dead and feel no comfort or discomfort.

5

The next day I arrived at my parent's home with the coffin, which I had brought in a van. My mother was sitting out on the veranda knitting a scarf and was surprised to see some workmen taking a coffin out of the van to carry it to the house.

"What is that?" she asked.

"As you can see, it is a coffin," my father answered from behind.

"Who is dead?" my mother asked.

"Nobody is actually dead," I told her. "Dad expects to die sometime soon and wants to have the coffin of his choice handy."

"What rubbish!" my mother shouted. "Take that ugly thing away from my house."

"Dad calls it a beauty," I said.

"However his distorted mind guided him to describe it," she said, "I don't want to see it in this house. Take it and dump it somewhere."

"But darling, I paid a fortune for it," Dad protested.

"Why were you sacrificing a fortune for a coffin when you are not dead?" my mother asked. "While you are alive, you need medicines, clothes, food, leisure facilities etc., and not horrible things like coffins. How on earth could you find a coffin beautiful? Are you an undertaker?"

"What is wrong with being an undertaker?" Dad asked.

"When our old British brothers were groping around for convenient family names, they went to all the professions to get them. They had Smith, Baker, Lawyer, Cook, Stevedore, Tailor, Woodman, Shoemaker, and even Underwood, but none of them ever imagined a name like Undertaker, so there," my mother said.

"But, darling," dad pleaded, "I will put it away somewhere and it will be brought out only when it is needed."

"No way," my mother said, firmly. "I won't have something in this house that keeps reminding me that you may die someday and abandon me alone in this world."

"If dad wants to die and abandon you," I said to mum, "don't panic for I will always be there for you."

"Who told you that you could ever replace your father?" mum said. "Take that horrible thing away. I simply don't want to look at it again."

"Where do I take it to?" I asked, confused.

"Sell it or give it out to some bereaved family that needs a coffin," she said.

I instructed the people who were carrying the coffin to take it back to the van. As we went to the van, my father followed.

"Keep it in your house," he pleaded "I really like that coffin."

"Mawumi will certainly reject it, too," I said. "Most women are afraid of coffins, even when they are new and empty."

"But you are supposed to be the man in your house," Dad said. "How could you allow your wife to throw out your dad's coffin? You know very well that I cannot give up my coffin just like that."

"It is not yet your coffin," I pointed out. "You might have paid for it, but it becomes yours only when you are buried in it. For now, it is just a coffin."

"I don't want to miss it," Dad insisted. "Try to hide it somewhere in your house."

"Your wife rejected the coffin," I pointed out, "and there was nothing you could do despite the fact that you are supposed to be the man in your home. I might also develop cold feet in front of my wife."

"But it is just a coffin," Dad said. "Beautiful and not cumbersome. You could hide it anywhere."

"There is no hiding place for a thing such as a coffin," I pointed out

Dad looked at me with pleading eyes. It reminded me of an attempt I once made to kill a rabbit for barbecue. When I held it by the long ears and brought out my sharp knife, it looked at me with such pleading eyes that I rather turned around and protected it from being transformed into a meal. Yes, dad's eyes were now similar and compelled me to develop the courage to face Mawumi with the coffin. However, I tried one lame attempt to dissuade him from insisting on keeping the coffin.

"Your wife may also have her own choice of coffin when the time comes to bury you and I will not be able to object." I said.

"I forbid you to bury me in any other coffin, unless something unexpected happens to this one," my father said.

"Unexpected?" I asked.

"You never know," he said. "The coffin is so beautiful that it might be stolen. Or a fire might break out. But make sure nothing happens to it. I won't be happy buried in something else."

I took the coffin home. Mawumi was hysteric when she saw it and attempted to block the workmen from bringing it to the house.

"What do we need a coffin for?" she asked.

"It is dad's coffin," I said simply. "He commands that he must be buried in it unless something unexpected happens to it before he dies."

"Then let the unexpected happen now," Mawumi said. "Take it back to wherever it is coming from and give it back."

"That is not among the unexpected things dad was thinking of," I said. "He was considering the possibility of theft or fire."

"I have added this other possibility that he might have overlooked," Mawumi said determinedly. "He is going to be buried as a dead man and whatever you bury him in will no longer matter to him."

"Would you go against the instructions of a most beloved father-in-law?" I asked.

Suddenly, I remembered a hilarious story by Tom Sharpe. The setting was in apartheid South Africa where a Boer police chief admired the English so much that he was determined to have the heart of an English man. Just then, an English man was hung for some crime I cannot quite remember, but I suspect he was guilty of giving a copy of the book "Black Beauty" to a kefir to read. To get this English heart from the condemned man, our police chief organized a team of heart surgeons and arranged to have a heart transplant, replacing his dirty Boer heart with that of the English man. Through some error, the doctors ended up with the wrong heart, a cold limp thing that must have come from a corpse that had been dead for more than two days, instead of the fresh heart from the gallows. Exasperated, the surgeons, who had already opened the chest of this police chief to replace his heart with the English heart, secretly agreed to stitch up without replacing the heart and to convince the chief that he was now functioning with an English heart. The police chief, who had been under anaesthesia during the fake operation, was convinced and was happier for the rest of his life.

Without realizing it, Mawumi had given me the solution I needed. Dad would live happily to the end of his days believing that I had kept the coffin of his choice somewhere in my house, just waiting for his corpse to be buried in it.

I took the coffin back to the shop and arranged for it to be taken back. In the process, less money was refunded, but I didn't mind. I was not the one who paid for it in the first place.

Three days later, my father came to my office and insisted that we stroll to the joint of the other day for a drink.

"I have too much work, dad," I said. "Let's make it some other day."

Dad insisted, so we left the office and headed for the booze joint. As we were passing by the undertaker's, dad suddenly stopped.

"What is my coffin doing there again?" he asked "I paid for it the other day and you were supposed to have claimed it. I personally saw your mother rejecting it when you brought it to the house."

"That is not the one dad," I hastened to explain. "You see, some of these classy coffins come in pairs for couples that love each other very much. You bought one the other day so this one, which was meant for the other half of the couple, is now on display for any buyer.

"In that case," dad said, "I will buy it, too. Let my wife also have a beautiful coffin like mine."

"But dad," I protested, "she is not interested in a coffin now. She definitely said so."

"That is not true," my father said. "She is simply scared of keeping coffins in her house, but your house is there. You will keep this one along with the other one."

"If mum is scared about keeping just one coffin in her house, how do you think Mawumi will accept two?" I asked "She has accepted to keep your coffin but may not accept the second one."

"You don't want to go quarrelling with your old man on a simple thing like a coffin," my father said soothingly. "And don't forget I paid for the other one. This time, it is your turn to pay."

"Okay, dad," I said, seeing an escape route. "I don't have money on me here. I will have to go back to the bank later to withdraw something to enable me pay for your wife's coffin, although she did not ask for it."

"Don't forget when you take it home, to put it alongside mine," Dad said. "I wish we could die at the same time on the same day."

"For that," I said, "you simply need to arrange a ghastly accident involving the two of you."

"Who told you that we want to die horrible deaths?" dad asked.

The next day, I passed by the undertaker's, admired the coffin a bit, and left without buying it. My next move, however, was to call dad and make his day happy by telling him I had already bought the coffin, taken it to the house, and placed it just next to his.

"Your wife had no problem with it, I hope," Dad said.

"I overcame her objection and she had to accept the second coffin, too." I said. "Dad, you owe me one."

For a week my dad did not border to call at the office but phoned every day to ensure that their coffins were safe. I kept assuring him.

One day, he burst into my office, looking angry.

"I thought you said you bought the other coffin?" he said.

"Is your wife dead and her coffin is not available?" I asked.

"Don't beat about the bush, why is that blasted coffin still there?" he shouted.

"Where?" I asked innocently.

"At the undertaker's." he said.

"Which coffin?" I asked again. "Ah! That blasted coffin. It has nothing to do with your beautiful coffin I hope."

"I am not in a joking mood now," Dad said dangerously.

"Father," I said, "I know you are not hypertensive but you may attract one of those old age diseases if you keep shouting like that."

"Now, tell me," he said. "What is my wife's coffin still doing there in that shop?"

"Who told you it is your wife's coffin?" I asked.

"It is the same coffin you were supposed to have bought," Dad said.

"It looks the same," I said, "but it is different. Your wife's coffin is lying next to yours in my house."

"I thought the pair was unique," dad said. "How come there are still others in the market?"

"You said it was very beautiful, remember?" I said. "Others who have already concluded that they are on the threshold of death probably got attracted to it, too, and asked for their own to be made."

"Are you sure of what you are saying?" he asked.

"Sure," I answered.

That weekend, dad came across to my house and I was surprise he did not have mum tagging along.

"She went to one of those numerous women meetings" he explained, "and I took the opportunity to come along and admire my coffins."

Dad might have given the impression that he had believed that the coffin at the shop was a different one, but I now suspected that he was not quite convinced. There were no coffins to show him to admire and I did not know what to say. Just then Mawumi came in with a glass of fruit juice on a tray.

"Here, daddy," she said, "Here is something wonderful for you. Full of vitamins and minerals".

"You want to kill me with diabetes?" Dad protested "Real men should not drink mush like that. Is there no whisky in this house, or have you transformed my son into a mineral water drinker?"

I saw my chance. Mawumi is a faster thinker than me and would know on the spur of the moment how to erase the intention of admiring coffins from dad's mind.

"Serve dad some whisky, dear," I said to Mawumi. "Look for the best. You know dad has class, and this high quality taste is well reflected in the class of his coffins that are in our keeping."

"You know it is a bit early, and mum frowns at his taking too much whisky," Mawumi said.

"A shot or two will not kill him dear," I said. "Besides, he wants to stay a bit and admire those coffins."

Mawumi was quite sharp and understood immediately.

"Ah, those coffins," she said "Yes, they are quite beautiful and quite matching. I will give you the whisky, but promise not to come requesting to see the coffins."

13

"Why?" Dad asked. "I simply want to admire them."

"You cannot admire them without me seeing the frightful things," Mawumi said. "I did not sleep for two nights each time Akoni brought a coffin home. Anyway, I had him put them away and lock them up. It will not be easy to climb up to that remote corner in the loft just to lug down heavy coffins for you to admire. Forget about them, Daddy. You will have time to admire yours when it is brought down, and that will only be when there is need for it."

She served dad with a liberal dose of Jack Daniels and cooed into his ears.

"Enjoy your drink, my greatest darling. You are aware of the fact that Akoni comes only after you."

The old man felt quite flattered and smiled happily.

"I have forgotten about coffins," he declared. "Keep treating me to good whisky and I will lose the capacity to remember coffins until it is time for me to be placed in one."

Mawumi poured him another dose, and this time I joined him. Drinking with company was certainly merrier.

"I hope he will keep forgetting about coffins until we have to put him in one," I said to Mawumi as we went to bed later.

"What really made him start thinking about keeping a coffin?" Mawumi asked. "I have heard about cases here in Cameroon where some parvenus buy and keep expensive coffins in which they hope to be buried, but I thought it was all excitement and naked pride. I never suspected Dad of such an absurdity."

"Even the idea of a family vault or tomb is quite repulsive to me," I said. "People spend huge sums of money preparing for their life after death, whereas the living are there starving and subsisting under the poorest living conditions."

"Did you read that article by Bulawa?" Mawumi asked.

"What does it say, dear?" I asked.

"He looks at situations in Douala town where you find many large poor families living under squalid conditions and crowded in tight mosquito infested rooms, whereas just across them, others live in opulence. A small family occupies a super villa with large spacious bedrooms, each of which could house ten of the poor families. The monthly budget for the kitchen alone comes to much more than the poor earn in their whole lives. While living in these castles with extra rooms that are never used, including several expensively equipped living rooms, these moguls also have large, sophisticated tombs in the village just waiting for their corpses to be brought and put inside to rot."

"Bulawa is right," I said. "What puzzles me, however, is why these poor families are always overpopulated as opposed to the rich ones?"

"Maybe poor family planning," Mawumi replied. "But I think it is because the poor are more open and receptive, and so they keep receiving family from the villages, who come in for greener pastures. The rich are not as accessible."

"Coming back to Dad's strange desire to have a coffin of his choice handy long before his death," I said, "there is a marked difference to those pompous fellows who construct lavish tombs and keep expensive coffins. Dad is simply interested in the beauty of the coffin."

"Are you suggesting that if Dad wanted to become a collector of something, he would go for coffins instead of stamps, old currencies, or some other odd collectors' item?"

"I don't see Dad filling up the place with coffins and considering them as collectors' items," I said. "In this case, his action is similar to choosing the burial clothes or attire in which you want to be buried."

"I once watched an interesting Nigerian film," Mawumi said. "A very rich man was suspicious about the way he would be buried because everybody around him was lusting for his gold. When he finally died and was buried, he resurrected to find out whether he had been buried in grand style or simply dumped away like a dog. To his dismay, he discovered that he had been buried in a very cheap coffin reminiscent of the types you found in old cowboy films, like the ones starring Clint Eastwood, Bud Spencer, and Terrence Hill. His family had struggled to keep all his money, believing that money was meant for the living to spend and that the dead no longer had any use for it. Besides, in the Bible, which is considered the greatest book, there is a declaration somewhere that we should allow the dead to bury the dead instead of fussing over them."

"If I met those relatives of this deceased rich man, I would stand them drinks for acting cleverly. I am sure that in his lifetime, this rich man was certainly greedy and made no attempt to help these needy relations of his."

"I thought as much too," Mawumi said.

"So, what happened?" I asked. The story sounded very interesting.

"You don't want to know how he managed to resurrect and come back to this world not as a ghost but as a man of flesh and blood?" Mawumi asked.

"That would be interesting to know," I replied.

"Well," Mawumi continued. "According to the film, this greedy old man had consulted a strong medicine man when he was still alive. For a large amount of money, he had secured a certain product that could bring you back to life after you died."

"The producer of that film certainly had ideas," I said. "But it means rich people would continue living forever because that product could always bring them back to life for another lifetime."

"Follow the story to the end," Mawumi advised. "This special potion was just effective enough to bring a man back to life once, and only for ten days."

"That is more comforting." I said. "So he used this stuff to come back to life for ten days. Did his resurrection not scare away everybody?"

"He came home with the strong medicine man of his who gave some sort of explanation to the relatives. He was kind of accepted back."

"And what did he do then?" I asked.

"He decided to use the ten days at his disposal to prepare for his own burial and death celebration. He bought a very expensive, imported coffin, which he kept in his bedroom. He even started sleeping in it just in case."

"Imagine the inconvenience of spending a whole night in a coffin," I said. "You are obliged to stretch out like a corpse. Anyway, the fool had been a corpse already and must have had the hang of it. What did he do next?"

"He bought cows, goats, chicken, yams, bags of rice, and lots of food items to guarantee that there would be a great party to send him off," Mawumi said.

"A send-off to hell, I am certain," I said. "Such greedy blokes always end up in hell."

"Where ever," said Mawumi. "He followed up the food with truckloads of wine, beer, and other assorted drinks. His idea was to convert all his wealth into items that would be used in giving him a hectic burial and funeral. He even arranged for lots of flowers, the most expensive funeral home and hearse, and things that he did not even need."

"What a greedy pig," I said. Oh, sorry pigs, I did not mean to spoil your name."

"He went to the church and paid a lot of money for the bishop himself to preside over his funeral mass," Mawumi said.

"He could have paid the church to protect him from dying again," I said sarcastically.

"After all these preparations, he died again on the tenth day," Mawumi said.

"Good riddance," I said. "So this time he left virtually nothing for his relatives to share."

"Not much," Said Mawumi. "But in frustration the guys too went to extremes."

"What extremes?" I asked. "The bloke had already converted all his wealth into items for his grandiose funeral."

"That is where they outsmarted him," Mawumi said. "The moment his eyes closed, the coffin was sold off and replaced with a simple one nailed up by a neighbourhood carpenter."

"That was ingenuous," I said.

"The next thing was to sell off all the animals, drinks, and expensive items that had been bought in preparation for a great funeral. Even the funeral service accepted to refund part of the money that had been paid to them and strike off their role."

"Mawumi," I said. "That is one film that ends well. I don't bother much about Nigerian films, but I am sure I will look for that one and watch it."

"I will see whether I can get a copy tomorrow," Mawumi said.

"Do you really think there is an afterlife?" I asked Mawumi.

"Belief in God talks about a choice between heaven and hell after death," Mawumi said.

"Why don't you think we all rot away just like animals?" I asked. "There is no proof to the contrary."

"From ancient history till today," Mawumi said, "all cultures and civilizations have treated the human being as different and virtually all have believed in a life after death. This has not been for nothing. There is the saying that there is no smoke without fire."

"Don't forget that in some cultures people were eaten just like common animals," I said. "Besides, there has been very little respect for human life. If you catalogue all the destructive wars, you will see that human life has meant nothing all along. People are simply killed in battle and left to rot."

"What of how most communities strive to bury their dead decently?" Mawumi asked.

Mawumi had a point there.

"Now that we have convinced Dad that his coffins are safe," I said, "we just have to keep it that way. Good night, dear."

"Good night," Mawumi said. "Let us come back to reality and think about the present, while leaving life after death in the hands of God."

She had raised another topic for discussion.

"If the idea is that we should forget about existence after death and leave everything to God, then we should not bother about things like the devil and hell." I said.

"We cannot fail trying to imagine how heaven is." Mawumi said.

"My idea of heaven is that it is simply a good place to be after death. You don't go to heaven through hectic funerals and lavish church ceremonies. The direct way to heaven is rather a good life on earth."

"Bravo." Mawumi said.

"Yes," I continued "If you live a good life on earth, you should have no worries about what is ahead. You should rather be worried about the people you leave behind, whether they have enough to thrive on, how they will bare your absence and what life has in store for them."

2

My office was located in a building at Ngvumissi Street in the Bochian neighbourhood. Our firm employed over a hundred of us, comprising managers and senior staff, clerks and secretaries, technicians and errand boys. Virtually everybody in the office knew my father through his frequent visits and the unending jokes he always had ready to share. The female staff in particular liked him for, despite his advanced age, he still looked quite handsome and was equally charming. I gave no heed to this as I was convinced that my father might mingle very well with females but had eyes only for my mother. Even when a buxom middle-aged and quite handsome female started talking fondly of him, I never suspected anything.

It was only when I discovered that Dad had come to our office on several occasions without coming straight to my office that I started wondering. Who else would he come to see? It was normal for him to stop and say hi here and there along the way to my office, or to smile flirtatiously at some of the pretty girls, but I though he always came to me right away. When I expressed my worry to one of my colleague, he exploded with a loud guffaw and rocked with laughter for a while.

"You mean you don't know?" he asked.

"Know what?" I asked perplexed.

"Your father has grabbed a chick here, man," he said. "He has developed some terrible infatuation for one of the females in this company."

"Which one?" I asked.

"Miss Jam," he said.

Miss Jam was the aforementioned middle aged woman. She was in her late forties and had never had the luck of marrying despite her good looks and the fact that she would have loved to be a wife. She had a daughter who was now married to a medical doctor in a nearby clinic. I did not know whether to believe my colleague about Dad's infatuation with Miss Jam, so I decided to feign ignorance about the relationship in front of Dad until he decided to open up to me. I got used to the fact that I was no longer Dad's sole target for visits in the firm. I held on like that for a while, but during one of Dad's now rare visits to my office, I was overtaken by curiosity and could not help broaching the topic.

"Is she not in today?" I asked.

"Who?" he asked innocently.

"Miss Jam, of course," I said. "Who else would you be looking for in this joint?"

"Yes, Miss Jam," he said. "Quite a charming lady."

"More charming than mum, I suppose," I teased.

He ignored my statement

"So you are already on to our secret affair?" he asked.

"What is secret about your relationship with Miss Jam? Who in this firm does not know?" I said. "You two have been careless about the whole thing. You have been acting like two excited school children."

"Are you sure?" he asked.

"If I had not blocked it," I lied, "your promiscuous activities here would have been transmitted to mum."

"I hope you will not be stupid enough to let your mother hear about this," he said "She would be terribly hurt."

"So you are aware of that?" I asked. "If you cared so much for your wife's feelings, you should have refrained from wagging your tail carelessly."

"Son," he said, "your mother is very caring and loving but no longer very exciting to make love with often. She keeps me starving at times. Jam, on the other hand, is a ball of fire. She has revived all the erotic flames in me and made me feel that I am a real man again."

"But, Dad," I said. "I thought at your age men no longer bothered about sex and just lay snoring by the sides of their old wives each night."

"Then you know nothing about old age," Dad said. "You need to see your mother in action when she is in the mood. If you could penetrate into the bedrooms of most couples over seventy years of age you would be surprised. If you were thinking of giving up sexual activities by the age of fifty, then you will certainly need a friend to help you along with your wife."

"Anyway," I said, "I hope your affair with this seductive lady will not stretch into real love and a desire to take another wife."

"The Church forbids that," my father said. "Besides, my marriage to your mother is monogamous."

"Which means you would have done it if these roadblocks had not been in your way?" I asked.

"That is careless talk, son," Dad said.

"Sorry, Dad, but I am still worried that this lady may end up as a much loved concubine to you, and that is equally dangerous. I might soon have Mum complaining that you sleep out."

"Now, don't exaggerate son," Dad said.

"Tell me, Dad," I said. "When do you have time to be alone with Miss Jam, given the fact that you have to go back home to your wife early and Miss Jam has work during the day? Don't tell me that you guys jump into the nearest inn for a quickie just like two young adulterers."

"We are not that old, you know," my father said, "and that is the only option. Anyway, our hotel has class, not one of those rundown inns. We are quite careful and always plan our encounters such that Jam is not missed at work and I am not missed at home."

"How would you feel if you imagined Mum in some other man's arms?" I asked.

"That is not something a man should ever think about," he replied. "You are also a married man, son, and I hope you are not foolish enough to ever imagine that your wife can cheat on you."

"That is one piece of good advice dad." I said.

"Such thoughts about the possible infidelity of the woman bring a lot of exaggerated jealously and suspicion on the part of the man and those are not things that should exist in a good home," my father said.

"Anyway," I said "I hope you protect yourself well because I don't want my mother to be infected with one of those dreadful diseases just because of your philandering. Sexually transmissible diseases are so rife, and you never know who is carrying them."

"So your worry is only for your mother?" he asked. "What about me?"

"You are the one who has decided to take the risk and go enjoying yourself," I replied. "When you go back home looking like a faithful husband, my mother, like a dutiful wife, innocently gives in to your sexual advances, as you have just told me. She does not deserve any punishment for being a dutiful wife."

"I see," my dad said. "I hope you are as faithful to your wife as you pretend to be."

"I am no philanderer, Dad," I replied. "And don't forget the possibility of making a baby at your age if you don't use protection while relaxing in those classy hotels."

The old man looked at me in an unfriendly manner.

"You are the first boy I have seen in my entire life that is not his father's ally in these matters but rather supports the mother fully."

"Don't forget that I am my mother's little boy," I said smiling.

"Whatever the case," dad said, "I am doing this to help your mother. She cannot keep up with my demands for sex and gets angry when I pressure her. She prefers it when she is in the mood and makes the first move."

"Are you telling me that at this age you remain a superman?" I asked. "I only hope you will not end up with cardiac arrest, and on a woman."

This time, the old man laughed heartily.

"Whatever you say," he said, "I know perfectly what I am doing. I take the steam off with Jam and get home sober and ready to patiently wait for your mother to decide whether she is in heat or not. Since I started this affair with Miss Jam a few months ago, your mother is definitely happier. You should thank me for that."

"She is your wife and you owe her the obligation of making her happy," I said, "although your method of doing it is deplorable."

"Not deplorable," Dad said. "It may be debatable, but I think such a debate will always weigh on my side.

"That is your opinion," I said. "I wonder whether Mum would accept that you could cheat on her to give her a little respite."

"Try to understand," Dad said. "I am keeping two beautiful women happy without hurting either of them in the process. Don't you see that what I am doing is an honourable thing?"

"You are hurting my mother," I said. "You are sharing out what is hers to other women."

"That is a stupid statement," he said. "To hurt a woman is to inflict physical or emotional pain, either deliberately or by error. I am not going out with other women but with one other woman. Further, I am rather keeping your mum happy. She is blissfully ignorant about my relationship with Miss Jam. As for this lady, Jam, she knows that I am married and is contented with the little time I give her. She has never complained and rather reminds me to rush home to your mother when she notices that it is running late."

"She might soon want more," I said, "and you will find yourself in trouble."

"Miss Jam is contented with my company during the day, and not every day at that. She also needs her own free time. She earns well here, and her daughter is married to a good man."

"Don't be deceived by that," I said. "Many relationships with women start like that and later on the women become gluttons. She might soon decide that she wants a child from you or that she wants most of your time."

"You are imagining things," my father said.

"Very soon, she will compel you to spend some nights with her," I said.

"I tell you, Miss Jam is not like that," Dad said.

Three days later, Dad came to visit me in my office, wearing a very beautiful shirt.

"That shirt is wonderful" I said. "And it fits you very well."

"Miss Jam bought it for me," Dad said. "She has eyes and taste. I tell you, that lady is a jewel."

"Has mum seen this shirt?" I asked.

"Of course," he answered. "I wore it in front of her this morning before living the house."

"Did you tell her where it is from?" I asked.

"I told her it was a gift from you," he replied, "Son, you need to thank me for that statement because it earned you lavish praises from your mother. She described you as a good son who knows what is good for his father. She even declared that this is my best shirt."

"Poor, innocent Mum," I said pityingly.

"You don't need to say that," Dad said. "You make me feel like a scoundrel and I feel so guilty."

"But you are guilty," I pointed out.

"Son," Dad said, "have you ever heard of a necessary sin?"

"And what would that be?" I asked.

"It is a falsehood, but not a crime," Dad said. "It is used in situations where all you want is to bring happiness or achieve a positive impact. You see, my relationship with Miss Jam has ended up making your mother happy in her ignorance. It has made Miss Jam happy, too, and made her to do good acts like the purchase of this shirt. Finally, the relationship has made an old man like me quite happy."

"I only hope you don't get caught one day," I sighed. "Now that Miss Jam has started buying you shirts, very soon she will have the audacity to start supplying your underwear and doing other dangerous things. Don't you see she is no longer satisfied with the finger and now wants an arm?"

"She could take the whole arm for all I care," dad answered. "The rest of my body is still there for your mother."

"After the arm, she will go for one leg," I said, "and then the other. The moment she creates an avenue, she will go for full ownership of what is generally known as the third leg. After that, Mum will have nothing else to live for."

"Look here, young man," Dad said. "I still love your mother very much. What I am doing with Miss Jam is just a sexual relationship. It can never go beyond that."

"I wish Mum were here to hear it," I said. "She would have clapped in happiness that her man will never abandon her completely for another woman."

"Don't be sarcastic," Dad said.

Two weeks passed and Dad only called for me once to accompany him boozing. We said nothing more about his illegal sweetheart. On a certain Thursday, however, he burst into my office looking worried.

"What is it, Dad?" I asked. "Woman trouble?"

"Who said anything about a woman?" Dad asked aggressively.

"For the past two weeks you have concentrated on Miss Jam and abandoned me, who has always been your old boozing chum," I said. "Now you come into my office looking like Job after God had allowed Satan to give him rough treatment."

Dad shuffled over to the cupboard where I kept whiskey and cognac, poured a liberal dose of cognac into a glass, and sat down. I was waiting for him to talk. He took his time though. Slowly raising the glass to his lips, he took a sip of cognac, which he rolled around his tongue expertly, savouring all the good flavour and taste before swallowing. His eyes glistened as the fiery stuff went down his throat.

"Something has come up that really worries me," he finally said. "Miss Jam insists that we must go on a weekend trip."

"I warned you about the possibility of wanting more and more," I said reproachfully.

"I was coming to you for a solution," Dad said, "not for you to be reminding me about statements that are past and gone."

"Why does she want a weekend outing?" I asked. "I thought she was satisfied with day-time quickies in expensive hotels."

"She said she wants to know how it feels to pass the whole night with me," Dad said. "How do I sneak off for a weekend and leave your mother alone?"

Both of us were quiet for a while, thinking. I could quite understand his predicament.

Suddenly, he brightened up.

"I will have to rope you into this so that it does not look suspicious," he said.

"I won't allow myself to be roped into anything fishy," I said. "I can't contribute in such a crime against my mother."

"But I told you before," Dad said, "this is not criminal at all."

"No way," I said. "You are trying to drag me into this quagmire of deceit and I am not for it. I will feel very guilty deceiving my mother."

"She is simply your mother, but she is my wife. My guilt should be greater than yours, except that what we are going to do is not that criminal."

I made an attempt to speak and Dad stopped me.

"We are going to explain to our wives that we are going out over the weekend for work. You are on mission, and I am coming along to help and keep you company. Then we grant Miss Jam's wish and take her along."

"Dad," I said. "I did not know that you were such a schemer."

"So will you go and convince the women that we are going on a working trip over the weekend?" he asked.

"No, dad," I answered. "I won't be able to do it."

"But, son," he said. "You are my right hand and the only person who can understand me completely. You are the only shoulder that I can lean on. You won't fail your old man at this crucial moment, will you?"

"I can't go on deceiving my mother to satisfy some female competitor," I said.

"Your mother faces no competition," Dad said. "Besides, I am also dying to experience the whole night with Miss Jam."

Dad looked at me with pleading eyes and my heart melted. You can't just stand like a rock in front of a pleading father, especially one who is your bosom friend.

"Okay," I said, "just one night."

"No problem, son," dad replied. "One night is enough. Thank you very much for that. What would I do in this world without you?"

"Simply don't push me next time to do this kind of thing," I said.

"Of course," Dad replied. "I am very grateful for this one night and should not bother you again."

Dad paused for thought for a little while.

"Come to think of it," he said suddenly. "Let's make it two nights so that I come back fully satisfied and have no reason to bother you again."

"Dad, you already declared that one night will be alright," I said.

"Two days will not kill you," he replied. "If we can stay out for one night, we can easily stretch it to two."

"That is not fair, Dad," I said.

"This is my only chance to have thorough satisfaction with this very appetizing woman," Dad said. "Please don't make me miss it."

"And my mother has been unpalatable all along?" I said. "So my mother has suddenly become sour because you have found honey in Miss Jam?"

"You have to understand my position," Dad said. "You are a man, and God has given men greater opportunities to sample a few nice babes while remaining fully satisfying to their wives."

The old man was now smiling.

"Dad, concerning this proposed weekend trip and your request for two nights; I think you are being selfish," I said. "You are thinking only about yourself. How do you think I will feel sleeping next door to you in the hotel and imagining you bouncing on that buxom lady?"

"Take a room at the other end of the hotel," Dad said. "That way you will sleep quite calmly and won't have to imagine things in the night. You would rather dream of your good wife and how, after missing you for two days, she will become a ball of fire in your warm arms on your return."

31

He smiled roguishly.

"Taking a room at the other end of the hotel and far from us has other advantages," he continued. "You could, for example, sneak in a lady without me noticing it. You know I love your wife too much to stand seeing you cheating on her."

"Are you insinuating that I love my mother less by being an accomplice to your philandering?" I asked, shocked. "Dad, this sacrifice I am making is not what a son who loves his mother would do happily. I am accepting under heavy pressure and stress."

"I simply want to protect your young wife and I have not said that you love your mother any less," Dad said. "Your wife is still young and needs all the action from you. Your mother, on the other hand, is on retirement from such actions and only needs a small dose now and then to keep her going."

Dad paused to ensure that everything he was saying was sinking in.

"I assure you," he continued, "that I never cheated on your mother when she was still young and you were growing up."

"How do I know?" I asked. "If you are doing it now, it is equally possible that you have always done it."

"So, two nights it is. We understand each other." Dad said conclusively.

What could I do? He was my dad and always had the last word.

"Dad, where do you get all the strength from at your age?" I asked.

Dad looked at me and smiled roguishly

"Anyway," I continued without waiting for an answer, "there is Viagra and all that stuff. If those Viagra producers only knew the havoc they were causing in people's homes, converting respectable old husbands who would have stuck to their wives into horny and capable lechers."

"Don't look at it that way," Dad said. "Consider the good Viagra has done for many old women who still wanted sex but their old men could no longer perform. Your problem is that you know very little about old women. They want their regular dose of sex even when they are quite old, and most of their men are not naturally up to the task. If you developed a good questionnaire and carried out an elaborate survey on old women in Africa and sex, you would discover that most of these old mamas turn to serious church going and meetings, and time consuming philanthropic activities, simply because the old man is no longer capable of giving them sexual satisfaction. What is more aching about the whole thing is that these same old men become active whenever they rope in a young girl. On the other hand, these wives are already too old to attract sexually capable young bucks and philanderers. Son, Viagra and sex enhancers bring back the desire and capacity to perform in the old men and our old wives no longer remain sex starved. Your survey would prove that sex enhancers are more useful to the women and help to keep old couples together."

"Dad, you are unforgivable," I said.

"Do you know why some men become passive homosexuals?" Dad asked.

I shook my head in the negative. I knew very little about homosexuals apart from the fact that they are attracted to partners of the same sex.

"It is simply because they want to enjoy sex but cannot easily rise to the occasion…"

Somehow, everything was concluded about our trip and dad believed, I am sure, that he had succeeded in putting me straight on the positive side of his affair with Miss Jam. We drove straight to dad's house and I took time to inform my mother convincingly about the impending trip.

She listened carefully and did not seem to have any real objection. She had no reason to doubt dad's reason for joining me on the trip and had all the confidence in me. At the end, she simply smiled.

"Are you sure you people have not arranged to go on a boozing spree where there will be no control?" Mum asked still smiling. "When there are two men away from home without female supervision, men who always enjoy the company of each other thoroughly, there is bound to be some degree of overindulging. I only hope you will have enough time to do the work you are going out for."

"This is pure work, Mum," I replied, trying to look serious. "I am not sure we shall even have time to sit down for more than a drink each night. I am actually taking Dad along because of the volume of work, although he is still hesitating to go."

This last statement was meant to clear off any bit of suspicion if there were any in the air. It was going to be quite a pleasure trip for Dad, but I suspected that loneliness and longing for my wife would compel me to drink as Mum was suspecting. I was really sorry that I had to be part of a conspiracy against this good woman, although I had been cornered into it

Mum turned to Dad, who was lolling on a long chair, reading a newspaper.

"You can't let your son down," she said firmly. "If he has a lot of work and thinks that you could help him, make an effort. Don't give lazy excuses. After all, there is not much that you have to do here over the weekend. If I feel lonely, I can go over to Mawumi and spend my own weekend there."

"I love my son very much," Dad said, "and would rush to his rescue any time. It is just that the thought of leaving you alone for up to two days really disturbs me. Anyway, you have Mawumi there to keep you company in my absence as you pointed out."

"Don't worry about me," Mum said. "Your son needs you so go and assist him. I will be fine with Mawumi."

"In that case," said Dad, "I will go along and give this young man the best assistance that he could get from any well-paid assistant. Though my body will be out there, my heart and spirit shall be back here with my dear wife. While I am away with Akoni for the weekend, your being with Mawumi will be quite a relief to me."

Mum was now totally convinced that we were simply going on a working trip. She went across and kissed the old liar fondly on the jaw. The old man smiled back, dragged her to himself and kissed her fully on the lips. Everything was now sealed.

Mawumi was somewhat disappointed that her weekend would not be with me by her side. However, she was consoled by mum's decision to come across and be with her during the period. Unlike many in-laws, they understood each other and enjoyed each other's company very well. Between the two of them, there was the true spirit of mother and daughter instead of mother and daughter in-law.

The next day we picked up Miss Jam and drove off to Fundong city for the weekend. Dad and his sweetheart were sitting behind holding hands and happily chatting away like newlyweds, while I was left alone in front. They looked like a happy couple celebrating their silver jubilee in marriage and every observer would have concluded that I was their chauffeur, taking them out on a second honeymoon. I turned on the music, not only to occupy and entertain myself, but also to muffle off the frequent sounds of kissing that came for behind.

After two hours of driving we finally got to Fundong city and booked into the Afo-a-kom Hotel, and there I made sure that I took a room far from theirs. After supper, we sat down for a drink. By the end of that first drink I felt like I was one person too much. I could guess that the two love birds were already wishing that they could have a concrete reason to leave me and go engage in what the trip had been meant for. I stood up.

"Dad," I said. "I don't know when you guys would want to retire to your room, but I feel like driving out and seeing how the town looks. I might run into an old friend or two."

"I hope you don't mean an old girlfriend or two," Dad said, "for I have to protect my daughter in-law fully. Anyway, you have been on my side all along so I can give a blind eye this once. Go enjoy yourself."

I thought he said these last words quite eagerly, almost as if he was hastening me away. I turned to move when Miss Jam smiled at me.

"We are no longer that young to go gallivanting around town at night, hopping from bar to bar," she said. "But do be careful and take good care out there."

I decided to tease a little.

"You are sure you don't want to come out with me and see the town a little?" I asked, already aware of the answer.

36

"No! No!" Dad said. "Old folks like us should retire early. Go and enjoy yourself son and good night."

"Good night," I said.

I left the two of them and went out. After several boozes, I came back to the hotel, went to my room, and slept soundly. When a man is out of town and not looking for mischief, the best way is to fill up the system with booze. You have a sound sleep, no tossing around in bed, no longing for the wife at home, and no unwanted dreams.

The next morning we all met for breakfast. As I came in cheerfully and greeted them, I thought the response I received did not come from a couple that had passed a wonderful night. I sat down and examined them closely. Dad was stirring his Kola coffee morosely, while Miss Jam seemed to be disgusted with the appetizing food in front of her. I was sure there was something wrong and that a tactful probe would bring it out.

"You had a wonderful night, I hope?" I said.

"We had a quarrel," Dad said. "Miss Jam almost abandoned me in the room last night."

"To go look for a real man?" I asked jokingly. "Dad, were you not up to the task?"

"I could disown you for saying that," Dad said. "You know your old man can still beat you anytime."

What could be the problem? A friend of mine once told me that love making is most explosive when you are cheating. In the company of a girlfriend, conversation is livelier and happier than with your lawful wife. This friend insisted that the only thing that could make two persons that were not legally married but had sneaked into a room for such fun come out disgruntled would be that the man had failed to live up to expectation sexually or financially. Besides, dad and his girlfriend had only two nights to exhaust their longing to be together for an extended period.

I was quite puzzled and decided that Miss Jam could explain better, so I looked questioningly in her direction. She had a subordinate position to mine in our work place, although my father's infatuation for her had made her feel free with me.

"What could be the problem, Miss Jam?" I asked.

"Your Dad snores terribly," she complained. "I could not sleep a wink and when I woke him up several times he got irritated and barked at me violently."

"That is not a big deal," I replied. "As a present this coming Christmas, I could offer him one of those nose contraptions they use to prevent bears, dogs, and other animals from biting. That way he could wear it each time you guys sleep out. The only problem there is that kissing would be impossible."

"That is not funny at all." Dad said coolly.

I was aware of Dad's snoring tendency. Out of excessive love for him, my mother had learnt to bare it. I am sure that his snoring now sounded like music in her ears. But here he was with another woman who simply wanted sex and would not want her sleep disturbed after a pleasurable bout.

"Which man does not snore?" my father said angrily. "Snoring is one of the traits of a real man."

"Some snoring could be tolerated," Miss. Jam said, "but yours is unbearable. Your snoring sounds like staccato gun fire from one of those outdated machine guns. How does your wife stand it, or do you sleep in separate rooms? "

"Don't talk rubbish, woman," my father said. "My wife has never complained about my snoring."

"I still wonder how your wife stands it," Miss Jam said. "Anyway, maybe she has no choice. If she had found a better man and a better sleeper, she would have abandoned you."

Dad simply glared at her and said nothing.

"Don't forget that we still have one more night," I reminded them. "With this kind of discord between you, how do you propose to sleep tonight?"

Dad remained silent. Miss Jam was stirring her tea.

"For this night, I propose you block your ears with cotton or block his mouth and nostrils with some material that can muffle the sound," I said to Miss Jam.

"I am not spending another night with this old man whose snoring is louder than the roar of Mount Vesuvius erupting," she said. "If you are not taking me back, I will look for my own way."

She looked very determined.

"Then," said my dad, "consider the relationship as over. I can't have a woman who keeps disturbing my sleep and complaining loudly about my snoring. I am sure I simply purred like a satisfied cat."

Internally, I was quite happy. Dad should go back and be faithful to his wife, meanwhile Miss Jam should go look for a widower or a bachelor who sleeps as silently as a mamba. I put on a sad face however.

"In that case," I said, "let's go home, Dad. We have to take Miss Jam back. From every indication, she will need some time to simmer down, and I don't think it will be out here in Fundong city."

"And what reason do we give for coming home one day earlier?" Dad asked.

"Leave that to me," I said. "I will tell them that the mission turned out to be quite easy and you missed your wife so much that we abandoned booze completely, concentrated on the work, and finished in record time."

I eyed Miss Jam to see how she was taking the conversation. It did not seem to mean anything to her; after all, as an old-time spinster, she had probably been in the game for quite some time.

On our way back, Dad had occupied the other front seat and during the two hour drive said nothing to Miss Jam. If Miss Jam had anything to say, she spoke only to me. I was driving happily, not caring whether there was music or not. I was going back to Mawumi and my mum, the two women I loved most in the world.

3

I did not see Dad for a whole week after our return from our fake working trip, so that weekend Mawumi and I went across to spend the Sunday with them. Dad and Mum were quite happy to see us, each for their own reason: Dad because he had a drinking partner for the day and Mum because she had a few gossips to exchange with Mawumi. I also had a secret reason for going there – I wanted to see how Dad was taking his rift with Miss Jam. Mum did not seem to have noticed anything, and treated her man with all the love and care as usual.

After lunch, we all left the dining table and went outside to a lawn where there were chairs and tables for our beer. The women provided snacks. Conversation went on as usual. Mawumi was telling us about some award her boss had received.

"That fellow should retire and rest like most of us," Dad said. "He is my age mate and he is still working. He should make way for younger men and women."

I poured drinks for everybody.

"He is still very competent and hardworking," Mawumi said. "You see that he is even receiving an award. And this particular award is not given just like that."

Mum surprised us at this point. She had remained silent for a while, munching away at some prawn crackers.

"That boss of yours is a very gallant fellow that any woman would admire," Mum said. "He is handsome, knows how to dress, and appears quite respectful and polite."

"And when has he been showing you all these wonderful characteristics for you to admire?" my father asked angrily.

41

He picked up his drink and sipped noisily to calm down his nerves

"Oh, don't be jealous dear," Mum said. "You know very well that we have often met with him in one social function or another."

"During which you might have wished you were married to him instead of crude old me?" Dad said stubbornly, sipping his drink again noisily.

"Akoni, tell your father he is acting like a jealous little school boy who is afraid of losing his first girlfriend and does not want to trust anybody," Mum said

Dad would not give up easily.

"You described him in such a way that any right-thinking person would draw conclusions," Dad said. "Handsome, elegant, and neat, for God's sake. That makes the husband sitting next to you to feel sordid, ugly, and crude."

"Dad! You are exaggerating," I said. "You know very well that Mum did not mean that, and you are hurting her very badly."

"It is good that you are a man like me," Dad said, trying to drag me to his side.

"And what about being a man?" I asked. "Is it supposed to make me less sensitive to the feelings of a woman who is very dear to me?"

"Son," Dad said, "I am sorry I reacted like that. The point is that honest men like me do everything to stick to their woman and remain very faithful to her. When she openly admires some other bloke, you are bound to feel jealous and hurt. Who knows what might happen or what might have happened behind your back."

Mum and Mawumi were quite embarrassed, but I knew better. Dad was simply ranting like that because of his latest escapade. It is generally said that lechers are the ones who worry most about the activities of their wives or daughters and interpret every word or action of theirs in a certain direction. Since lechers often had their way with many of the women they went after, it was normal to believe that, if these women could give in to them, their wives and daughters could equally be very vulnerable. Dad is not such a wonderful lecher, but his recent affair with Miss Jam and Mum's innocent indifference to everything might have made him jittery.

"Dad," Mawumi stepped in "you are acting like a naughty boy and we, the women, could sanction you for that."

"Well said, my daughter," Mum said. "We could start by clearing away the drinks and abandoning you and your son."

"You see, Dad?" I said. "You have trifled with the gentle sex instead of handling them like breakable stuff."

"It just came out like that, son," Dad said. "I am sorry."

"Rather direct the apologies to your wife," I said. "You have to realize that you are a very lucky man. Even Othello would trust Mum completely, and deep inside her heart, she believes that you love her like Romeo loved Juliet."

Dad relaxed and smiled.

"Son, I did not know you were that strong with Shakespeare's works," he said. "I thought that, apart from your office work, the only other thing you did was to admire your wife or drink."

"Don't escape from the point at hand," I continued. "This woman is golden and should be treated with all the respect and care in the world."

"That is a chip off the old block," Dad said, congratulating me. "Very soon we shall start competing over the love for your mother."

Dad turned to Mum.

"Mia culpa," he said in Latin. "You are the best thing that ever happened to me, and you know it."

"The apology is accepted, but it is not complete." Mum said. "You hurt a few of us."

"You simply cut me short." Dad said. "This young man here cannot be struggling to get closer to you than me, your husband, without me also struggling to get closer to his wife than him. Mawumi, will you forgive me, or should I say it on my knees?"

"Why don't you go on your stomach?" I said.

"I wish some people would keep their big traps shut while I am talking to my darling daughter," Dad said. "Mawumi, would you allow this bloke to come between us?"

"Certainly not, Dad," Mawumi replied. "You are number one. He can only come in second place, or if you prefer, we could push him further back and place the children before him."

Everybody laughed and the atmosphere relaxed.

After the laughter, there was calm for a short while. We were waiting for someone to bring up another topic for discussion. However, I was surprised when it finally came from Mawumi.

"Dad," Mawumi said. "Are you not a staunch member of the Anlahsi club?"

"Why do you ask?" Dad said. "We have been there together on several occasions. I am even the one who sponsored your husband there."

"I was just saying, Dad," Mawumi said, "that I did not see you there when we had a seminar with the members last month."

"Was your husband there?" Dad asked.

"The meeting mostly concerned retired persons who happened to be members of the club."

"Yes, I remember," Dad said. "When I saw that you were listed as one of the speakers, I decided to stay away. Retired indeed! All those old men are far from retired."

"Why, Dad?" Mawumi asked.

"Why are they far from retired?" Dad asked.

"I want to know why you stayed away when you saw my name on the list of guest speakers."

"I did not want to see my favourite daughter in-law ridiculed by dirty old men," Dad said. "Those old men no longer have anything to lose and can be very crude and vulgar. At times, when I sit there for a drink, I wonder where the world is heading to."

"Dad is right," I said. "Often we hesitate to take our decent wives out there."

"And take your girlfriends?" Mawumi teased.

"If I proposed to take you to the Anlahsi club for a drink, you would be the first to hesitate," I said.

I was also a member of the Anlashi club and had noticed a lot loose talk there.

"That is a club designed for the leisure of honourable gentlemen," I said, "but what transpires there is worse than what you would expect in one of those joints where they sell native liquor. There is lots of rotten language, and the old chaps openly go for any female around, married or not. Viagra is openly sold, and ideas on how to get a hard on easily freely hawked. To cover all this up the motto of the Anlahsi club states; what you see, hear, and observe here should stay here when you go out."

"I am sure that when you go there you guys also loosen up and have a go at the loose language and the few available women."

"Certainly not," I said hastily. "We simply try to enjoy our drinks and pick up hints and ideas. The female members and other women who come there are often real boozers. They are used to that kind of male company. They enjoy all the bawdy jokes and fully participate. They openly accept requests for sex and openly comment on members with whom they have had previous sexual encounters. They applaud those who had performed wonderfully or condemn those who had been a disappointment. At the same time, these females easily reject any advances from unwanted males without any qualms. Many of the women are not married."

"Anyway," Dad said, "how did your talk go? I hope the old goats were quite happy to receive a talk from a great woman like you."

"They asked very embarrassing questions," Mawumi said. "If I had known that it would be like that, I would never have accepted to present that talk."

"Were the questions they fired at you accompanied by obscene gestures? Dad asked.

"I did not notice any," Mawumi said. "Maybe I was not very observant. But would it be normal for gentlemen of such a prestigious club to stoop so low?"

"At old age, many males become as rowdy as little kids," Dad said. "You mean they did not openly admire this pretty face of yours and wish they could have you?"

"There was some insinuation in that direction," Mawumi said. "But I think I knew how to handle it. There was a particular bald fellow who kept insisting on a practical demonstration with the condom."

"Why would he want you to demonstrate how to wear a condom?" Mum asked. "Is there anybody in that club that has never used condoms before?"

"We had been given these wooden phalluses to use, but I did not think it would be necessary," Mawumi said. "The bald coot in question, however, was insisting that I should join him to demonstrate to the others how a condom is used in the sex act with a woman."

"You told him off in no uncertain manner, I hope," Mum said.

"I would have landed him a slap if he so much as touched me," Mawumi said.

"That's my girl," Dad said. "My son chose like his father. Congrats, Akoni."

"You see men," Mum said to Mawumi. "You do the right thing and your father in-law is congratulating Akoni."

There was general laughter at this statement.

"I ended up being applauded by that gang of toughs," Mawumi said.

When we got back home, Dad's reaction to Mum's positive statements about her boss were still lingering in Mawumi's mind. As we got into bed she immediately broached the topic.

"Why did Dad react like that?" she asked. "I smell something fishy."

"Don't go fishing for reasons that do not exist," I said. "It was just a spout of jealousy. He loves his wife too much."

"That is not a positive way of loving a woman," Mawumi said, "and it was strange of Dad. Would you react like that if I gave an honest positive assessment of one of your friends?"

"You try," I said, "and I will conclude that you have had an affair with him."

We both laughed at the joke as I used the remote control to switched on the TV. I was searching for a news channel. Suddenly Mawumi scratched me on the back and the sensation was so good I turned round hoping for the best. But I was stopped midway.

"Do you know what?" she said.

"Say on," I replied in disappointment.

"Mum informed me when we just got there yesterday and were preparing the meal that, since your trip, Dad has changed back to what he used to be."

I now became very alert. Something big might be coming as a follow up to that statement.

"You mean she had noticed a change in him before that?" I asked. "Dad has looked the same to me all along. You say Mum noticed a change?"

"Sure," she said. "A woman's instincts, I should say. Before your trip, Dad had been leaving the house more often than usual, although it was always during the day time and he never stayed out late."

"Was there anything wrong with that?" I asked." You know he often comes to my office."

"Mum and I both know that," replied Mawumi, "but the frequency suddenly changed. Besides, at times a woman may hesitate a bit before giving in to an insistent husband in bed. During this same period, each time Mum hesitated a bit to give in, Dad immediately turned round and snored off, leaving her rather frustrated."

"And what does that indicate?" I asked, fearing the worst. "At times a man could simply be tired."

"That was certainly not the case. This attitude of quickly giving up each time his wife hesitated to give in could mean anything," Mawumi said. "It could mean that he had come home tired as you say, or that his infatuation for her had dropped. It could even mean that he had been with another woman and assuaged his sexual desire, and was now simply trying to perform his marital duties, hoping that Mum would spare him the task by refusing."

This is just what I feared.

"And which possible explanation did Mum go for?" I asked, worried.

"There are certain things we women overlook just to have peace of mind and peace in our homes," Mawumi said. "Mum decided to go for the possible innocent reasons why Dad was acting like that."

"Thank God," I said, "that you are both reasonable women and understand that Dad is not a philanderer. If he had been one, this would have been uncovered long before this."

A man must protect his fellow man, even against his own mother, especially if the person protected is his dad.

"Maybe," Mawumi said. "But after your trip, Dad has come back fully to his old self. He hardly leaves the house, even to visit your office, and has started insisting in bed when he wants sexual satisfaction."

Women! They had noticed things all along but given no hint about their observations. It only shows you what women can connive and do. Men are simply lucky that their mothers and their wives hardly ever end up as close as Mawumi and my Mum. In most cases, there is discord between the two, making it impossible for them to put their heads together and chastise men for their numerous transgressions.

Two days later, Dad bounced into my office dressed like a young man of twenty five, in jeans trousers and a colourful Tee shirt. He was smiling broadly and looked quite happy. He went straight to the cupboard where I kept the liquor and poured himself a good measure of cognac.

"Dad," I said, "if you are coming for us to go out for booze, I cannot make it today. I simply have a lot of work."

"Who said I am coming for you?" he asked "I simply stopped by to say hi to my favourite son and gather some Dutch courage by sipping a bit of his wonderful cognac."

"Where are you heading to?" I asked with concern. "Have you found another Miss Jam? I don't think it would be prudent to go for another female in this same joint."

"Not another one," Dad said. "I have come to fix it up with my Miss Jam. Is this not a happy world?"

I was dumbfounded. I had thought from their last quarrel that the two fellows were completely unsatisfied with each other and nothing could bring them back to the status of sweethearts. I immediately changed my mind and decided to drag him out for a drink.

"Dad," I said, "we need to talk. Let's go and have our usual drink."

"I thought I told you that I did not come for you," he said. "Besides, you said you had too much work to do."

"The work can wait," I replied. "There is much at stake here. Let's go for that drink."

"If you insist," Dad said. "Miss Jam can wait a little."

I dragged Dad along to one of the joints and sat him down with a Kadji beer. I took my own bottle and sat next to him.

"Dad," I said, "you can't be coming to see Miss Jam. Your relationship got severed when she realized that you snore and you realized that she was impatient and intolerant. What do you want to do with her again?"

"I want to make things up with her," Dad said. "I enjoyed my brief stay with her and have developed some longing to sleep with her again."

"Be careful, Dad," I warned.

"Don't be afraid, son," Dad said. "There is no feeling of love in this at all. It is just a longing. Simply a desire to squeeze those ample buttocks of hers. I simply have to go and make it up with her."

"You would look cheap, going back to beg her, given the way she ticked you off," I said.

"Who is going to beg?" Dad asked. "She realized that she had thrown away gold and called me. She is already eager to see me and to apologize for her shortcomings of that day."

"She took the risk to call you when Mum could have been close by?" I asked.

"She just had to take that risk," Dad said. "She had missed me very much and had realized that she had made the greatest error in her life by falling out with me."

"And you cheaply fell for all that?" I asked. "Be a man, Dad, and reject her. You never know. She might have treated you like that on that day because she had an alternative guy waiting. Maybe the guy has suddenly chucked her and she has no option but to bounce back."

"Reject her?" Dad asked. "When she called me, I suddenly realized that I had been pining for her all along. I had no option but to accept to come and see her. Tell me what you brought me here for because I am already itching to go and see her."

"I still insist that it is possibly because no man wants her that she is sticking to you," I said.

"That woman can make love, boy!" Dad said. "And she is wonderful company. Any right thinking man would want her."

Dad sipped his drink.

"But you can't go back to her, Dad," I said. "Mum knows everything."

I watched carefully to see his reaction.

"You went blasting your whistle like a scoundrel?" Dad asked. "I suppose you could not resist telling your wife, who must have passed it over to her. I thought I could rely on you."

"That is not it, Dad," I said. "What I mean is that, through what Mawumi calls the female instinct, Mum was suspicious that you were having an affair."

"How could she have been?" Dad asked. "She never caught us and never complained."

"She might not have caught you red-handed, but certain things you did, or failed to do, got her convinced that there was something amiss. If Mum did not say anything, she was just being a brave and loving wife," I said.

"Phew!" Dad exclaimed.

"By observing your frequent movements out of the house and comparing them with your reduced attention to her in bed, she put two and two together and kind of deduced that something fishy was happening."

"Did she tell you all this herself?" Dad asked.

"No," I replied. "She confided only in Mawumi and Mawumi finally thought I should know."

Dad was quiet for a while.

"Dad," I said, "you should really reconsider this situation. I think Mum has been hurt enough."

"Did Mawumi say anything else?" Dad asked.

"She did, and this is very important," I replied.

I signalled the bar man to serve us some pieces of grilled chicken.

"She wanted me to know that women have a sixth sense and at times simply pretend to be ignorant of what is transpiring just to maintain peace in their homes," I said. "She explained to me that women are quick to realize the change in the usual attention they receive in bed and can easily guess that an attempt to lure them into sex is either eagerly done or done with reluctance just to cover up."

"Your mother noticed something there?" Dad asked, frightened.

"She did," I replied. "But, the good woman that she is, she avoided stressing you out and faced everything bravely."

"Why did she not say it, then?" Dad asked. "All along I thought I was satisfying her thoroughly."

"You were mistaken, Dad," I said. "If you go back to Miss Jam, things might end up very badly this time. She simply suspects that there was something wrong and has no idea about Miss Jam. I suppose we don't have to stretch things and eventually get Miss Jam into the scene."

"Let's have two more beers on me, son," Dad said. "Forget about Miss Jam and forget about whatever work you have in the office."

4

It was Dad's birthday and Mawumi and I had decided to invite him and his sweetheart to a classy restaurant for lunch. We had put aside enough money for this and were prepared to provide a very lavish meal. Mum had proposed an Indian restaurant, based on nostalgia for some dish called Tandoori chicken that she had eaten once while in university. For the occasion, therefore, we ordered Tandoori chicken, which was served with chapatti. For dessert, we were served some messy mango stuff that tasted awful. The Indian restaurant had been Mum's choice, but apart from the chicken, Dad and I didn't enjoy anything. I wonder whether Mawumi enjoyed anything else either, but she had this solidarity with Mum.

By the end of the meal, our taste buds had rather been fouled by the dessert, something probably made from raw mango that had been chopped up into bits and pounded into a messy pulp before adding vinegar and some horrible tasting spices

"To make this a real birthday," Dad suggested, "we had better migrate to some decent place where we could have Shashlik and good wine."

"What is Shashlik?" Mawumi asked.

"It is another name for Shish kebab," Dad said. "You will like it. It will repair all the damage that this Indian restaurant has caused to our taste buds."

I was quick to throw in my support for the idea before Mum raised any objections.

"We are supposed to be celebrating," I said, "so no need to rush back home without actually having the kind of thing that we like to eat."

Mum still insisted on raising an objection.

"We have already had a meal and I don't want a drunken husband back home on this special night."

"Give us a chance, too, Mum." I protested. "Mawumi and I also need as much time as possible with Dad on his birthday."

I looked towards Mawumi for support but none came so I had to struggle alone.

"Mum," I continued, "you were longing for Tandoori chicken and we have obliged you. On the other hand, Dad and I were dreaming of Shashlik and it is only fair that we have a chance to dig into it, too."

"Who talked about rushing back home?" Mum said. "I was simply cautioning your father to go slowly on the booze. I am enjoying myself thoroughly with all of you."

We were all surprised at her reaction.

"A friend of mine had talked a lot about Indian food, and I remembered the time I had sampled it in university," mum continued. "I thought for this special day we should have something out of the ordinary. Unfortunately, I rather seem to have ruined what was supposed to have been a very happy birthday meal. Let's go for the grilled meat and wine."

She turned to Mawumi.

"My dear girl," she said. "Today we will not allow the men to enjoy the good wine alone. We shall have champagne for ourselves."

We were all happy with Mum's reaction, and Dad and I were now comforted with the fact that there would be no serious restrictions on our drinking.

We moved to an open bar owned by a Caucasian where there was Shashlik and good wine from Armenia and Georgia. We sat down and ordered, and the company became merrier. As the women chatted happily and Dad and I knocked down the booze, I noticed that an elegantly dressed old lady sitting with some elderly fellows at a table not far from us was concentrating on our table. I wondered whether it was Dad or me that she was admiring. It could have equally been my mother's dress, hat, or hand bag. Women would openly admire anything on another woman and my Mum was an elegant dresser. Suddenly the old lady got up and moved towards our table.

"You are Ngongnuwi, right?" she asked, without pointing.

I was kind of flattered. For such an elegant lady to be interested in you means that your name and reputation might have gone further than you thought.

"Do you know me?" I asked "Because I can't make you out."

"I could not be addressing a young rascal like you," she said. "I am rather talking to that old hound in the horn-rimmed spectacles." She pointed at Dad.

"Njung Ngongnuwi," she said to Dad. "Is this presumptuous fellow your son?"

I noticed Dad smiling stupidly. He must have been old chums with the bawdy dame.

"Who is this lady that is taking liberties with my son?" Mum asked, the mother hen, coming to the rescue of her chick.

"Oh!" the lady from the other table said. "Is this your lovely wife? I heard that she is quite a piece of cake and I agree with that assessment."

My father was still smiling stupidly.

"Sorry for butting in, my friend," she said to Mum carelessly, "but this big rascal here happens to have been my classmate and my sweetheart, too. It is just that he developed cold feet along that line and scampered off."

Mum must have been confused because she gave no response to this provocative statement.

"You should have seen us in school," the stranger continued. "I used to bully all of them."

"You have left your own sweetheart over there," I said to her, pointing at the table from which she had come. "One of them could be your husband or boyfriend, and I think he is worried that handsome men like Dad and I have drawn you across like magnets."

"Ah, those," she said. "Those are my brothers and quite harmless. No man has been bold enough to marry me so I have grown up a tough old spinster."

She turned to Dad.

"I am still available though in case you regain your manhood, abandon this weak female by your side, and come back to me."

She dragged a seat from the next table

"May I sit down?" she asked. "I noticed that none of you was gentlemanly enough to offer a lady a seat."

"Just go back to your table, you troublesome woman," Mawumi said.

"On the contrary, let her sit with us," Mum said. "The bigger the crowd, the merrier. It is just that those men over there might feel bad because of the unceremonious way she abandoned them."

Mum stretched a hand to the new corner.

"Hello and welcome. We were celebrating Njung's birthday. He has been such a wonderful husband and deserves the best."

"Congrats," the other woman said to Dad.

"You said you were childhood lovers and you scared him away?" Mum said. "How could you let go of such a wonderful man? That was the greatest mistake that you ever made in your life because, now that I have him, I won't let him go."

I never expected such strong stuff from Mum. I am sure Mawumi, too, was certainly surprised. I looked keenly at the intruder, expecting to find annoyance on her face. Instead, she burst out into raucous laughter and carelessly patted me on the back. I was sitting next to her.

"Who wants that old retired stallion?" she asked, laughing some more. "Keep him for yourself. I had rather go for this young buck. I am sure he still has much energy in him and can cope with my exigencies."

"Newu will never change." Dad said. "She used to harass everybody when we were in school and did not fear even teachers. She was quite pretty though, and even now age has not quite taken its toll on her."

"You have finally opened your mouth," Newu said. "I thought you had become dumb now that you have a wife and even a son to speak on your behalf. And who is this other cute little girl, a second wife?"

"You know that I have always been weak and cannot cope with more than one wife," Dad said.

"Who knows?" Newu said. "When some of you old blighters can no longer be stimulated by your worn out wives, you look for young hot females to bring up the fire in you. Anyway, this one does not look quite hot."

"This is my son's wife, Mawumi," Dad said.

"So this cute young man has already been saddled with a wife?" Newu said. "Young man, you did not have to hurry like your father. When we were young, and I was still taking a little time to decide whether I should marry such a bum, he rushed off and got married. Now you can see that his wife is nowhere near me. I thought I could replace your father with you and drag you into my arms. Now I find out that some girl had already lured you into marrying her. What a shame. I will be compelled to go look for some other old classmate."

"And remain sex-starved because the tired old boy will not be strong enough to cope with a tigress like you?" Dad asked.

"I wonder whether there is any weak old man these days," Miss Newu said. "The market is now flooded with sexual stimulants, and old chaps are operating as if they were in their twenties."

"Newu," Dad said. "Where have you been all this while? If you have changed, it has been for the worse. You have become much more of a rustic than a barmaid, and I am not surprised that you have frightened all possible suitors away from you. I hope you have a child at least?"

"Who would have wanted to carry a big stomach around the place for months?" Newu asked. "Men do nothing for the baby to come, apart from enjoying themselves in sex, and then they step in and name the baby after themselves. Let other women like this, your gentle wife, have babies for I personally am not interested."

60

She looked at my drinking glass and frowned.

"What is that stuff you are having?" she asked.

"Cabernet," I said. "And the women are having champagne. Should I serve you some?"

"You want to serve me now because I have called your attention to it," she complained. "What type of gentleman would sit by a lady and wait to be asked before he serves her a drink? Your father has certainly passed on the gene for being very slow to you."

"I thought you said my father was rather too fast and got married to some other woman before you could make up your mind."

Miss Newu frowned at me.

"I am sorry," I said. "Will you take red wine?"

I looked round the table.

"Or champagne?"

"I don't go for things like that," she said. "Give me cognac or vodka anytime."

I called the waiter and ordered her drink.

"Bring her a bottle of Courvoisier," I said to the waiter.

"So," Dad asked, "Apart from scaring away suitors and interrupting people's birthday merriment, what else do you do in life?"

"I write books," she said. "Don't tell me you have never come across any of my books."

"Never," Dad said. "Are the books worth reading by people like us with refined tastes, or are they full of obscenities?"

"I would have bashed that ugly head of yours with this bottle of cognac if it were not for the fact that I am the one drinking from it," she said. "My books are popular and of the best taste. Have you ever read the book 'The Queen and her Boyfriend'?"

It is an extremely popular book, a bestseller. A bit on the raw side, but quite interesting to read. However, it carried a masculine name as author.

"You couldn't have written that book," I said. "It may sound like the kind of stuff you would write, but it bears the name of a man and not a woman as the author."

"What do you know about names?" Miss Newu asked. "I simply used a pen name. Many books are bought by males, and they wrongfully believe that men write better books. I simply used a penname to penetrate and I succeeded." She took a sip from her glass and put it down,

"I have made so much money that I could even replace that ugly suit you are wearing with a beautiful and expensive one," she said to Dad. "Is it your wife who offered it to you as a birthday present?"

Mum seemed to have adjusted to the prankish conversation of Miss Newu and did not seem to mind.

"With so much money, you came scrounging on our meagre birthday booze?" Dad asked, smiling broadly to show that he was joking. "When will women like you ever learn how to give, even in their hour of plenty?"

"I gave you freedom when I dropped you like a hot brick several decades ago," she said. "Isn't that enough generosity? Otherwise you would never have had the chance of meeting and marrying this wife of yours whom you seem to like very much."

"Don't you rather think that I am lucky not to have remained with you?" Dad asked.

"I am sure this weakling you have gotten married to is really what folks call the gentle or weaker sex, always at your beck and call, and you could spin her around like a yaw yaw."

"You are trying to get my wife to fight," Dad said. "But let me assure you that it is a vain effort. Now drink the cognac that has been generously offered to you by my son. If you can't finish the bottle, you are free to put it in your handbag and take it home."

There was a burst of raucous laughter again as Miss Newu beckoned the waiter and ordered five rounds of drinks for our table, excluding the cognac.

"Let me drown you and your family with booze before I leave," she said. "Njung, don't go missing again. Here is my card. Call me anytime you need good company or if menopause influences your wife to starve you in bed."

She stood up to leave.

"And young man," she said to me, "thank you for the cognac. That is what you should be drinking."

She moved off.

"What a character," Mum said.

"Dad," Mawumi said, "is it true that you two were lovers and could have gotten married?"

"No way," Dad said. "We were quite intimate. I was her protégé. As your mother in-law just said, she is of a strong character and a big bully. Most of the boys were actually afraid of her."

"She gave the impression that you were sweethearts," Mawumi said.

"Before I met your mother-in-law and married her," Dad said proudly, "virtually every female I met was attracted to me and wanted to marry me. Miss Newu was no exception. I was really a handsome and seductive guy in those days. I tried to pass these qualities on to my son, but it was not possible for him to have them all. Anyway, he ended up attractive enough to lure you."

"I suppose you must sing your own praises," Mum said. "One can easily see how you and this scandalous woman were twin souls. Maybe I should bring out the list of very potential males that would have given up their last dime to make me their wife, only for me to refuse all of them and end up with this empty vessel here."

There was no animosity in the exchange, which rather provoked much laughter from us.

"We should celebrate Mum's birthday in this same bar," Mawumi proposed. "Maybe some schoolmates or childhood lovers of hers will turn up."

"Mawumi," Dad said reproachfully, "I thought you were my sweetheart and always on my side."

"Dad will break any blighter's head that comes claiming to be an old classmate or lover of Mum's," I said.

"No, no," Dad said. "I would rather offer him a drink."

"And slip in rat poison to silently finish off the fellow," I said.

"How did you guess son?" dad asked, laughing. "Any blighter who comes insinuating that he knew my wife before I met her does not deserve to continue living in the same world with me."

"You see how jealous men can be?" Mum said to Mawumi. "His old girlfriend came prancing around like a hen in heat and doing everything to prove their past relationship, and he seemed to enjoy everything, not even bothering about my feelings. I wish one of my old admirers would come around."

Dad pretended not to be listening and instead asked me to pour him a tot of cognac. I obliged and he sipped it like a connoisseur.

"What can beat good cognac?" he said.

"Let's go home," Mum said. "We have had enough for one day."

I called for the waiter and settled the bill.

Back home, as we were relaxing, I remembered the incident at the bar.

"That woman really embarrassed Dad," I said to Mawumi. "I wonder how some women can be so rowdy."

"I thought those were the kind of women you guys prefer," Mawumi said. "Are they not better than dull women like Mum and I? And the way she drank. She virtually knocked down half of the bottle of cognac before abandoning it, and despite the fact that she took it dry, she left looking quite normal. I am sure she smokes cigars, too."

"Were you observing her that closely?" I asked.

"She actually looked like, if given a chance, she would pounce on you," Mawumi said. "Despite the impression she gave that she was joking, a woman does not take such chances."

"You mean, even in front of an old woman like that, you are not sure of your position," I asked.

"These days, every woman holds on to her man if she happens to have a good one and does not allow snatchers like her to have their way."

"She simply looks like a jovial old woman to me," I said. "And she is a famous writer. Her books are all bestsellers."

"What can that woman write, short of pornographic literature?" Mawumi asked.

Three days later, Dad came to my office, and I offered him a seat, but he shook his head.

"Work has ended for the day, son," he said. "Newu is inviting us to the Anlahsi club."

Dad normally did not need to be invited to sit down in my office. He always made himself comfortable as soon as he came in and his refusal to sit down betrayed his eagerness to see Miss Newu.

"You can't come in here and close my office for the day," I protested. "I still have lots of work to do."

"Not when there is merry-making with Newu," Dad said.

"But you could go alone," I pointed out. "After all, she was your classmate, not mine."

"Now she has become our mutual friend," Dad said.

"Are you afraid of her?" I asked. "When it was Miss Jam, you always sneaked off to meet her alone. Now that it is Miss Newu, you seem to be afraid of the possibility that she may drag you by force into one of the toilets of the club and rape you."

"Newu is not like that," Dad said. "She may be a bit crude with her language, but she is a decent woman. On the other hand, she drinks like a man and makes good company."

"I suppose she is the kind of woman for the Anlahsi club," I said. "I would like to see her taking on those old blokes who distressed Mawumi during her lecture."

"She could certainly take them with her left hand," Dad said.

I dropped everything and we took off to the Anlahsi club.

"Call your Mum; tell her that you are with me and that we are going to be a little bit late," Dad said.

"Should I tell her who invited us?" I asked.

"At times I wonder whether you are really my son," Dad said. "What a silly question you have just asked there. If I didn't have full confidence in your mother, I would have started doubting."

"Sorry, Dad," I said.

Miss Newu was perched on one of those high stools at the counter smiling at us as we came in. She came down from the stool and took us to some soft chairs.

"This is what soft people like you need, not hard stools," she said.

She was drinking cognac.

"What should they serve you?" she asked Dad. "Booze before greetings."

Dad opted for cognac too

When she turned to me I followed suit. She called and the waiter brought a bottle of Martell.

"You want olives, groundnuts, or any kind of snacks?" she asked.

"Whatever you offer," I said.

"So you young bucks also go in for stiff cognac, eh?" she said conspiratorially. "Along with the cognac, you could add a dose of Viagra so that you go home and make twins with your lovely wife this night."

Dad and I could not help laughing.

"Here they sell Viagra along with the drinks," she continued, "because many members are tired, weakened old bulls like your dad."

She seemed to suddenly realize that Dad was sitting next to her and listening.

"Njung, how have you managed to live without me for all this while?" she asked. "It is close to twenty-five years since we last met, right?"

"About that," Dad said.

"I was not there to protect you, yet you survived."

"You underrate me," Dad said.

"And you even have a family, a grown up son," Miss Newu said.

"I have not been sleeping," Dad said.

"So who has been sleeping? Me, I suppose," Miss Newu asked.

"Maybe," Dad said, "although I can see you give all your time to writing books."

"Is she a writer?" one old man sitting close by at another table asked.

"And why are you eavesdropping?" Miss Newu asked. "And up to such a point that you even have the audacity to stick your dirty nose into what does not concern you. I will soon have that ugly nose of yours bloodied."

The old man was taken aback by her reaction.

"Who does this female think she is?" he shouted back.

"And she thinks she can crow freely where only cocks are supposed to crow?" the old chap's companion said in his support. "A hen can never become a cock."

"I might have seen that face here before," said the former speaker, "but she appears to be new in town and does not understand that respect for the male is imperative here."

"Ignore them," Dad advised Miss Newu. "We have not met for ages and should rather be catching up on lost time."

She seemed to understand.

"Tell me more about your books," I said.

"What else can I say," she said. "They are all bestsellers and have been translated into many different languages. They are all being transformed into movies, too."

"How great," I said.

"My millions are calculated in dollars and generally give a whopping amount when converted into Francs."

"And you enjoy all that fame and money all alone?" Dad asked.

"That is not fair. You should have brought in a man to share in all that."

"And end up with a houseful of children, too, I suppose," Miss Newu said. "And possibly have an imposing partner with whom I would have to consult before I do anything? No thanks. I enjoy my money with my little Chihuahua and Pekinese. They enjoy everything I enjoy and never complain or impose."

"I am sure you give much to charity," I said.

"What for?" she asked. "If any beggar is out there waiting for my money, he is deceiving himself."

She laughed out loud.

"I am quite serious about it, so don't think I am joking," she said. "I contribute much to nature conservation though, quite a lot, but I don't give to the poor."

"Why?" Dad asked. "Giving to the poor is an act of charity. You help God by helping the poor."

"I will not promote laziness," she said. "No lazy bum will shirk work and other efforts to make a living and expect to have access to a drop of my money."

"There," I said, "you have the wrong notion of what we call the poor. This is a class of people who have been made poor by God, or should we say, nature? Out of no fault of theirs, they have no talent, have disturbing disabilities or have no access to any means of production. Some of these people even work hard and produce, but all of this is appropriated by unscrupulous land or factory owners, or unscrupulous middle buyers who have money and direct access to the lucrative market."

There was sudden clapping from Miss Newu.

71

"Young man," she said "If you look at it like that, you will never live well. You will share everything you have with them and remain with nothing for you and your pets."

"Would you consider mere pets more than human beings?" I asked. "Some of you rich fellows need your heads checked. Your pet's budget for a week is more than what about ten overpopulated poor families live on during the same period."

"You can't blame us," she said. "We love our pets dearly and have no feelings for these poor blighters. We don't even know them."

"At least you support nature conservation?" Dad asked.

"Yes, and that concerns me directly," she said. "I need to breathe good air, and my pets do, too."

"I wish you had a virile man to occupy you," Dad said. "You would not talk so much about pets."

"But you escaped from me and ended up with that dull woman, who does not even seem capable of knocking down a glass of good brandy. Where did you pick her up? The convent or some remote village?"

"That is my mother you are talking about," I reminded her.

"And as for you, young man," she said, "I thought that, having missed the father, I could grab the son. You are not that good-looking, but I could have managed with you. Then I discover that you had already rushed off and gotten hooked to an even duller woman. What is wrong with you blokes? Can't you wait a bit for the right woman to come along?"

"I am sure those dumb pets are what you should really have as companions," Dad said. "They can't complain, and simply have to wag their tails at whatever absurd command you give them."

Miss Newu burst into a loud cackle. Her hoarse voice made it sound sexy.

"Hey, I love that raucous cackle," Dad said. "I always developed a hard-on whenever I heard you laugh like that."

"Have you developed one now?" she asked. "We could simply bribe this young man with a bottle of good brandy and take off to some nice corner. An old he-goat like you should know many such corners."

"I thought you had given your life up to your pets. Why cheat on them?" Dad asked.

I stretched out and gave dad a pat on the back. I liked the question.

"Are you sure you are still capable of having a hard-on?" Newu countered.

"What should have taken it away?" Dad asked "I have a lovely wife who keeps awakening the fire in me."

"Are you sure you are not rather dreaming about me each time you make love to her?" Newu asked.

"If not for the fact that I have made enough money myself, I would have come after your millions," Dad said.

"There, you would have to fight with my pets, the Chihuahua especially," Newu said. "He can be quite jealous."

"Tell me," I said. "Many lonely and sex-starved women go for big dogs such as German shepherds or Saint Bernard that can effectively represent a man. What can you do with tiny Chihuahuas and Pekinese?"

"What do you know about dogs?" Miss Newu asked. "The small ones are better. They have good tongues."

Dad rocked with laughter for quite a while.

"Ah, Newu, Newu, you will never change," Dad said. "I wish I could have you every day for company."

"You have me now," Newu said, "so make the best out of it."

Newu signalled the bar man.

"This bottle is empty" she said. "Don't you see that I am sitting with two thirsty blokes? Instead of admiring me, they are concentrating on the bottle. Bring another one."

"The bottle is only slightly more than half gone," I pointed out.

"Possibly," Newu said, "but it means that it will soon be empty and will have to be replaced."

"Let us come back to serious talk," Dad said suddenly. "You may not help the poor directly but you could help them through the church."

Newu smiled.

"The church?" she asked. "Why should I use my hard-earned money to build churches?"

"If you were very religious," Dad said, "you would have accepted with me that the worship of God should be done in nice, decent places if possible."

"And now that I am not religious at all?" Newu said.

"You could still pass through the church to do charitable work," Dad said.

"I won't trust any church with my money," Newu said.

"You may be right when it concerns small Pentecostal churches where the Pastor mighty easily divert the funds," Dad said. "But the old, established churches are well organized and accountable."

"I still do not trust them," Newu said.

"These churches have hospitals and health centres, schools and institutions of higher learning, centres for the disabled or physically and mentally impaired, and lots of other very helpful institutions," Dad said.

"These are simply business enterprises," Newu said.

"OK then," I said. "Intervene through village development organizations, or even directly. Carry out projects like road improvement, access to clean and reliable water, scholarships to poor students etc."

"It is more rewarding to carry out these projects and help communities than to store the money in a bank and compete with others to be known as billionaires," Dad said. "Money was meant to be spent, and once you have guaranteed a comfortable life for you and your Chihuahuas, you could use the rest to make other people happy."

I suddenly noticed that Newu was thinking seriously.

"My son here could help direct you on how to go about it, but don't go enticing him instead," Dad said.

"You could set up a foundation," I said.

"Yes, I think we should discuss it seriously," Newu said. "This old rascal here could double as your mother's caretaker and the manager of this foundation. But mind you, Ngongnewi, the slightest misappropriation will result in me cutting off that joy stick of yours, and your wife may be left stranded."

"When do you think we can start then?" Dad asked.

"Not so fast," Newu said. "You should not be in a hurry to start swindling my money. This young buck here has to explain everything to me first,"

"That is normal," Dad said.

"Let us take a date then," I said. "Where and when do we meet?"

"Why not this night in your bedroom?" Newu said. "We could simply send off your woman to go sleep with her mother in-law."

"And what happens to me then?" Dad asked, laughing

"You would then be free to go out and look for a whore," Newu said.

"That was a good one," Dad said.

"Young man," Newu said, "meet me here tomorrow. Let us discuss everything while sober, before we drown ourselves in cognac. Don't bring this jealous old man along though. Who knows, we might end up in some nice hotel room."

"I won't allow you to rape my innocent son," Dad said.

"Very soon, you will tell me he is a virgin," Newu said.

"Time?" I asked

"Midnight," she said. "Oh, I forgot I was taking an appointment with a baby, not a fiend. Ok, meet me here at 3:00 pm."

"Come prepared to fill us up with choice cognac," Dad said. "This is an important meeting."

"Were you part of the meeting?" Newu asked him. "I don't remember inviting you to any meeting."

"I have officially been appointed as manager of the new Foundation, so automatically I have a place in this discussion," Dad said.

"Anyway," Newu said, "poor old blokes like you always look for the slightest opportunity to squeeze nice things out of generous rich persons like me. I won't mind having you clinging on to your son's tail in a bid to have access to good cognac."

"Son, make sure that you work on the budget, too, tomorrow," Dad said. "You won't forget to put half the resources as salary and allowances for the manger. Add a Rolls Royce, too, as my service car, and a small executive jet if possible."

"I did not know you were such a dreamer," Newu said.

The next day, Newu was already at Anlahsi club when Dad and I arrived.

"Hello, young men," she said.

"Did you call me a young man? Dad asked.

"I simply wanted to flatter you a bit," Newu said. "Beside your son, you look much like the elder brother of Methuselah."

"My son is that young and you wanted to rape him yesterday?" Dad said. "You would rape a new born baby boy if you had the chance."

"Another statement like that and I will send you back into the job market," Newu said. "Yes, I will simply give you the sack."

"I am sorry ma'am,." Dad said. "I am sure you would rather rape a male Chihuahua."

"That is even worse," Newu said. "For that statement, I could cut off your source of cognac completely."

"OK," Dad said. "Let us make peace. I don't intend to lose my juicy job of manager, especially as it is my son that will determine my salary, my allowances, and all my benefits or amenities."

"Njung Ngongnewi," Newu said. "You are a lousy old man, but I like you very much."

Dad smiled.

"That is the spirit," he said. "It is always good to be liked by nice old women, especially rich ones."

"I have not finished, you dirty old man," Newu said.

"There was something else?" Dad asked. "Soon you will say that you love me more than anything else in the world, even cognac."

"I like cognac very much," Newu said, "but I like your son even better."

"Wait a bit," Dad said. "Are you declaring that you like my son better than me?"

"He is young, energetic, and handsome," Newu said. "Whereas you are old, exhausted, and wrinkled. Women always like good things, you know."

"Even old, expired hags?"

"Who is an old, expired hag?" Newu said. "I hope you mean your wife."

"Akoni!" Dad said to me. "This woman keeps picking on your mother, and you accept bribes of cognac from her?"

"She is your wife," I said. "Why don't you defend her?"

"I can see that the bribe has really worked," Dad said. "Newu, do you realize that you have corrupted my son into forsaking his mother?"

Raucous laughter resounded from Newu's lips.

"Let us get down to work," I said. "You old chaps should forget about your past love affairs until we are through with this."

"OK," Newu said. "We are with you. If this rogue disturbs us again, we shall banish him from this club, and I think I will follow it up by disinheriting him."

"You got that, Dad?" I said.

"Why don't you concentrate on your work?" he answered.

I turned my attention to Miss Newu.

"Foundations are very common in Europe and America," I said. "Rich individuals like Ford or rich couples like Bill Gates and his wife become aware of the fact that they have much more money than they need. They therefore set up a foundation through which the excess money is used for charity."

"Hey, I am nowhere near these guys," Newu said. "They are heavy weights, valued in billions of dollars, while I could be valued only in millions."

"That is just the problem," I said. "You see, at that level, where they keep competing to be among the top ten richest persons in the world, they hesitate to deplete their bank accounts by giving too much to charity."

"Yes, once up there, one strives to remain there and remain among the billionaires," Newu said. "Who does not want to figure each year as the world's richest man or woman?"

"You now see that when it comes to donating to charity, you could easily beat them to it." I said. "You could become famous and popular as the top donor to charity."

"You see, Newu," Dad said. "The monthly budget for one Chihuahua could be transformed into a project that could make a whole community happy."

"Don't stretch to my pets," Newu said sternly. "I won't compromise their happiness just to please some gooks that I don't even know."

"Dad did not mean that," I said. "Your pets are like your family and you must provide for them. Give them whatever they want - canned food, beer, tooth brushes, and even underpants. But you see, that will take only a small fraction of your income. We are talking about this bigger part which keeps coming in but which you can't consume."

"You have put it better than your clumsy Dad," she said.

"I will soon ban you from seeing this woman," Dad said.

"Don't worry, Dad," I said. "I am trying to pave your way into getting a good job."

"Forget about that, old boy," Newu said, "and let's concentrate on our work."

"Thanks ma'am," I said. "Now, some Foundations are all-round. Others concentrate on scholarships for poor students. Others prefer to provide schools, while some concentrate on health facilities or water. There are many domains of intervention."

"What of gender aspects?" Newu asked.

"Emancipation and empowerment of women is one of the main destinations of such funds," I said.

"We could concentrate on that then," said Newu. "There are many horrible men like your father who use tradition, culture, and societal norms to suppress women."

"Could I suggest something?" I asked.

"Go ahead," Miss Newu said.

"I propose we add to this the aspect of water," I said. "It is normally women who fetch water and who use it for washing and cooking."

"That is OK," Miss Newu said.

"Then, we have the aspect of health," I said. "Women need it most and are the ones that are most concerned when babies and children fall ill."

"I accept," Miss Newu said. "What next?"

"Since you are already into nature conservation, we add that to the activities of the foundation." I said

"I did not know that Njung could have an offspring that could reason slightly better than a sloth," Newu said. "Next step?"

"We determine how much you would sacrifice each year for the foundation," I said.

"That is where I come in now," Dad said.

"We work out management and personnel costs," I said, ignoring him. "We then identify the projects we intend to carry out for that year. It may be necessary for certain projects, like water, to carry out feasibility studies and develop project proposals."

"Thank you, young man, for introducing this to me. I am sure I would prefer to make a name through acts of charity than to make a name through the size of my bank account."

6

There was a knock on the door and I went to open it.

"Who is it, dear?" Mawumi asked from the dining sector. The cling of forks and spoons rang out as she prepared the dining table for lunch. The noise came from the cutlery of stainless steel that she was picking out from some tray she was carrying and placing on the table.

"Some lunch time visitor." I said, smiling at Dad, who was standing in the door way. "It looks like we have a hungry visitor coming to share our meagre food ration for the day."

"It is simply some hungry fellow who knows that you prepare good food and has come to sample a bit of it," Dad added. "Your husband may be a good man, but it is not fair for him to continue enjoying all the good food alone."

"Oh it is you, Dad," Mawumi shouted back. "Come on in. Your place at the table head is always guaranteed."

Dad came in smiling.

"Just on time," he said. "While driving across, I was afraid that I might arrive a bit late, just to find out that Akoni had already wolfed down everything."

Dad moved straight to the table and sat down, admiring Mawumi as she went to the kitchen and brought out the food.

"That is really a pretty lady," he said. "I did not know you would be capable of making such a good choice. I had almost thought seriously of choosing a woman for you."

"Dad," I said. "Don't admire my wife that much or your own wife might get jealous and angry, and if a fight starts between you two, I will certainly support my mum."

"Your mother appreciates Mawumi's beauty too," Dad said, "and she has taste and flair for good things. When your mother says something is nice, the statement cannot be challenged."

He turned to the dish that had just been placed in front of him.

"Chicken," he said, "and well prepared by a master."

"A master?" I asked. "Mawumi is a woman."

"Mistress would not go," Dad said. "These are the problems foreigners face with the English language where the masculine dominates. Yet they claim to have equality among the sexes."

Dad picked up the serving spoon and began to serve himself. He took all his time without considering the fact that I might have been famished and longing to dig into my food.

"I hope this husband of yours did not go for the gizzard while you were still cooking," Dad said. "To us old African men, the gizzard alone is the whole chicken."

"It is right there, Dad," Mawumi said.

"You are free to have your gizzard and leave our chicken to us," I said to him.

"You don't mean what you are saying," Dad said.

"I mean everything I am saying," I replied, smiling.

I turned to Mawumi.

"Please, help Dad locate his gizzard," I said. "But make sure he gets nothing else. Reserve the rest of the chicken for us."

Dad pushed Mawumi's hand away as she attempted to serve him, selected some juicy chunks for himself, and put them on his plate alongside the gizzard."

We all laughed, served ourselves, and went ahead to eat.

"I did not only come for this lunch," Dad said after several mouthfuls. He always enjoyed Mawumi's cooking.

"Then why are you imposing yourself on our meagre resources?"

"Mawumi is a wonderful cook and I would not miss her food any time I have the chance."

"What brought you here then?" I asked. "And without my gentle mother at that."

Dad loaded chicken into his mouth and smiled happily.

"I want to remarry," he said simply.

I almost choked on the food I was trying to swallow at that critical moment. I thought I had not heard correctly, but Dad went ahead to repeat what he had just said.

"Yes," he said. "I wish to remarry."

"Remarry?" I asked. "What has Mum done wrong?"

"You cannot be seriously considering the possibility of marrying another woman," Mawumi said.

"I am remarrying your mum you block head," he said to me. "Who else would I be getting married to?"

He possibly realized that Mawumi, too, had been led to think that he had been talking about marrying another woman.

"I am sorry, Mawumi," he said, "but it is your husband that I addressed as block head."

"You actually scared me," I complained.

I poured Dad some more wine, refilled my cup, and turned to my food. Mawumi hardly drank wine so I did not bother to pour some for her.

"Dad," Mawumi said. "You need to explain a little more what you mean by the statement that you want to remarry, and to a wife with whom you are already married."

"It is quite simple" Dad said. "Your mother and I got married abroad where there were only a handful of guests and very few gifts."

"You regret the way you married?" Mawumi asked

"Of course," Dad said. "All these years we have attended hundreds of lavish marriages with lots of wedding presents pouring in. We may be old, but I am longing to sit on a high stage with my wife and become the great dignitary of that day."

"You could be the laughing stock of the year Dad," I said.

"On the contrary," Mawumi said. "If we plan and organize it well, you may find every old couple in town trying to do the same thing."

"What would this old boy do without you?" Dad said to Mawumi. "A couple with a lot of style like mine cannot do a thing like that and other old boys would not want to copy."

"Who will be the groom's men and bride's maids?" I asked. "Many of your age mates have already grown out of shape. Their suits and dresses will not fit."

"I was rather thinking of you as a page boy and Mawumi as a flower girl," Dad said.

"You can't be serious, Dad!" I protested. "I am already more than forty years old with children who are in their teens."

I imagined myself in one of those tight suits and a bowtie, looking like a naughty and hungry page boy who is already fed up with the ceremonial part of the occasion and is eagerly looking forward to eating cake and having a glass of orange squash at the reception party.

"Think how interesting it would be," Dad said, as if he were reading my mind. "You in a tight page boy suit looking like a naughty juvenile and Mawumi with pigtails, dressed in one of those girlish gowns and carrying a basket of flowers."

Dad smiled broadly.

"And I, decked out in one of those swallow tail diplomatic suits with my beautiful bride clinging to my left arm."

"Dad, you are dreaming," I said.

"Anyway," Dad said. "I want us to plan it well. We can leave the church part to your mum and concentrate on the reception party. Where do you think we should have the reception?"

I thought for a little while.

"We could do it in your home," I proposed. "There is enough space outdoors to arrange chairs and tables.

"I want a big thing," Dad said, "not some small house party."

"What of the Anlahsi club then?" I asked. "It is spacious enough and every event there is well publicized."

"That could go," Dad said. "And they have good music, too."

"Mawumi will look for the catering service to hire," Dad said, "and you will handle the rest. My wife and I will just sit back and wait for this great day."

"Wait a minute, Dad," I said. "I need the names of those you want to invite. Then leave the rest to me, apart from the bills."

"Son, I want everything to be big and I intend to spend lavishly. Your financial support will not hurt though."

"Did you rob a bank?" I joked.

"You should put in a lot of money into this," Dad said. "It is like an investment. After all, most of the gifts will end up with you."

"Wedding gifts cannot be relied on," Mawumi said. "You may end up with a cheap collection of beer glasses, tea cups, trays, cheap cutlery, and some cheap wall clocks."

"That is when young folk are marrying," Dad said. "For a classy old guy like me, only the best will come in."

"What date are we talking about for this great event?" I asked.

"A month from now," Dad said.

"Have you discussed this with Mum?" I asked.

"You know that your mum and I are two hearts that beat as one," Dad said. "She hesitated initially and protested about high costs, but I assured her that we had enough money. I brought out my situation in one of the banks where I had been saving money just for the occasion. I made her understand that we could equally have strong external support, especially from a vibrant son like you."

"Dad," I protested. "You can't count on my meagre income for this grandiose scheme of yours."

"Don't worry, son," Dad said. "You will only step in when I run short."

"I hope you don't plan to run short too early and leave me to foot most of the bills," I said.

"Mawumi," Dad said, "your husband is afraid that I will squander all the money he would otherwise inherit."

"Just give us full access to your bank account and you will have your wedding party," Mawumi said. "By the way, how much are you giving to the church? You know that these days the church insists on its share before blessing you to go spending lavishly on others."

After the meal, Dad insisted on a glass of cognac.

"After a sumptuous meal like this one it is necessary to accelerate the digestion process," he said.

"Maybe we can discuss some details while digesting," I said. "Let's move over to those reclining chairs."

"Son," Dad said. "Your mother is getting more beautiful each day."

"That is good to hear, Dad," I said. "It probably means we shall never have cases of Miss Jam again."

"No, son," Dad said. "That was a fleeting weakness. Your mother is quite alright for me."

"I hope that day arrives soon for you to prove it."

"Which day are you talking about son?"

"The great day, of course," I said. "The day on which you shall marry mum again."

"Ah, yes," Dad said. "I am looking forward to it myself."

"And Dad?"

"Yes, son?"

"I hope on this honeymoon you guys will make another child like you did during your first honeymoon."

"Have you forgotten that we are retired senior citizens?" Dad asked

"It is just that I have always longed for a junior sister," I said, laughing.

The next days were quite busy for me. Beautiful, expensive invitation cards were printed and distributed. Apart from Dad's friends, I included a number of mine so as to have company of my own age. I selected the music to be played on that day and helped Dad select his suit and shoes.

At the level of entertainment, I arranged for the venue to have the right décor and ensured that assorted drinks of all sorts were made available. We had more assorted drinks than the Anlahsi club itself had ever displayed, even during club night.

The great day finally arrived. We had chosen well and Dad's suit was a wonderful piece that made the old fellow look like Prince Charming. Mum was resplendent in a magnificent robe that Mawumi had helped her to choose. Her makeup was exceptional and her hairdo was something any woman would admire. The prince might have made an error and gone for Mum if she had been present in that ball where Cinderella was destined to be the beauty of the night and capture the prince's heart. Apart from the exquisite outlook, Mum's smile brought out all the hidden beauty in her. I am sure all the old chaps that had been invited to the occasion were filled with admiration. Smartly dressed, Dad probably caught the eye of every female in the hall.

The occasion started with an elaborate church service. Tickled by the ample amount that my father had paid for the church service, the reverend gentleman spared no possibility of making the occasion look like mass on Christmas day. He had pressured the choir to practice well, and special songs had been composed. The church itself had been wonderfully decorated and the priest himself came out with an outfit reserved only for such occasions. It was certain that apart from the large amount that Dad had given, alms collection was going to be hectic. All the rich old men and young dynamic fellows in town were going to be present and would certainly donate heavily.

At the end of the church service, we all took photographs in front of the church. Everything was done just like in a normal wedding. We then moved to the Anlahsi Club hall. The car that was conveying dad and his wife had been hired.

It was one of those American Limousines that are absurdly long but prestigious.

At the Anlahsi club, the official part was quite brief. I had insisted on very brief speeches and this was respected by all except dad. Anyway, it was his day so we had to bear it. Besides, the speech was so interesting that everybody wanted it to continue.

This remarkable speech started thus:

"Old boys and old girls, children, grandchildren, and great grandchildren, you are all welcome to this marriage ceremony and thank you for coming. I remember somewhere in the Bible where a rich man organized a feast like this one, and issued out invitations to his neighbours, far and wide. He invited everybody that mattered, just like all of you seated here. Eh, I hope nobody is standing. Anyway, what happened was that virtually all the key invitees developed some alternative program at the last moment and could not come. What a shocking disappointment to the host when they all simply gave excuses to cover their inability to attend the banquet. This would have completely ruined the whole feast. The astute host immediately thought of the strategy of inviting every passerby so as to fill up the banquet grounds and to ensure that all the food and drink he had prepared were consumed and not wasted. Despite the fact that this motley crowd he ended up with in this famous banquet was handpicked at random, and not given any time to prepare or dress up for the occasion, the host still ended up severely blaming one of them for not dressing properly. Thank you for abandoning wives you have just married, cows you have just bought, your fields and commitments, and your pretty newborn sons to attend our occasion. And properly dressed, too."

Mum was smiling radiantly by his side. For best man, Dad had chosen my son and for the chief bridesmaid, they had settled on Mawumi's kid sister. The two teenagers looked a bit embarrassed from their position at the high table in front of virtually all the high dignitaries in town.

Dad cleared his throat and continued.

"During this unique gathering, you will learn from us how to marry properly, so we invite all the young hopefuls here to watch closely."

Dad stopped and surveyed all the booze lavishly displayed in front of him and on each table in the hall.

"Marriage is a day of happiness and feasting, highlighted by giving lavishly to the couple who are marrying so that they can start life properly," he said, receiving heavy laughter from the guests in return. They were all aware of the fact that Dad was not a poor man.

"In the Bible, Jesus' first miracle took place during a wedding ceremony," Dad continued. "Yes, he changed water into good wine so that the guests should have enough to drink. Jesus was simply a guest, but he provided enough to keep the wedding going. And he provided high quality stuff. He did not give grudgingly. I call on all of you here to follow his example when you are attending marriage ceremonies like this one. If you notice that there could be a shortage of drinks, act up and provide just like Jesus. I challenge you all to be ready to do like Jesus, who, like you, was a mere guest in this wedding ceremony in Canaan. When he noticed a shortage, he acted promptly by providing. It is true we cannot perform miracles like Jesus whom we are told simply changed water into wine. But the wine shops are there in their numbers, open and always ready to sell. You simply need to dig into your wallets and things will go accordingly."

I thought this was the foulest speech I had ever heard from a groom during a wedding ceremony but the guests reacted otherwise. It took quite some time for the applause to calm down so Dad could continue.

"Thank you," he said, looking much like Obama during his inaugural speech. "Now, we are through with the aspect of drinks and are certain that many of you will be watching out for any shortages so that you replenish like Jesus did. Let's go to the other aspect, food."

Dad turned and looked at his wife for inspiration.

"Although it was not during a wedding ceremony, Jesus fed thousands using only five loaves of bread and two fish," he said. "Satisfaction here was partially psychological. The people decided that the food was enough and delicious and went away with that in mind. We have here much more than five loaves of bread, but is it enough? On the other hand, all of us here could make up our minds like the crowd Jesus fed in the Bible and leave here greatly satisfied with whatever we are served as food. Whether you eat to your fill or not, leave here with your mind made up that you have had all that you wanted to eat and in ample quantities."

I was wondering where Dad had dug up all that crap, but he seemed to be saying just what everybody wanted to hear. Marriage speeches have often been dull, with the guests praying for a brief one so that they can go on with their feasting. In this case, however, they seemed to be enjoying it.

Dad had not yet finished.

"What I have been trying to say," he continued, "is that we should all leave here very satisfied. I challenge all my mates to remarry but not with anyone else apart from their wives. That way we will all have banquets like this one to attend virtually every weekend."

Dad smiled broadly as there was more clapping.

"There is a time in life when a wife's attention is torn between the husband and the children. That stage goes away when the children are grown up and have become independent, and all her attention reverts back to you. For your part, you must equally make your wife the centre of your life. I wish to solemnly declare here that my wife is the centre of my life. Any lady in this hall who has the intention of wooing me or enticing me because of my good looks should forget it. I am fully attached to this woman here, and I advise all husbands present to stick to their wives. I think the priest was clear about that in church."

When Dad sat down it took some time for the applause to stop.

By the end of the occasion, despite the fact that Dad was a bit soused, some of his old chums insisted on following him to his house that night for a night cap.

"We want to make sure that he goes straight back home with you instead of sneaking off to one of the charming old dames who were openly admiring him in the hall," one of them explained to Mum.

"I am supposed to go back home alone with her so that we rush into bed and consummate this remarriage," Dad said laughing. He was actually in favour of his close chums tagging along for a night cap.

We thus transferred to Dad's house. As I bustled around trying to see that everybody was served, the old fellows were chatting and laughing happily.

"My woman is so pretty and enticing this night," Dad suddenly said. "I might have made an error in allowing all these male hawks to follow us to the house."

Dad turned to a corner where the women that had come along with their men had chosen to sit.

"Ladies," he said to them. "I am sure your horny husbands wanted a chance to continue admiring my wife and claimed that they were simply coming to see us off."

There was general laughter.

The next day Mawumi and I went across to see how Mum and Dad were fairing after their remarriage.

"Dad will certainly still be in bed nursing a hangover," I said to Mawumi as we moved up to the house.

"Dad could not be that stupid," Mawumi said. "On such a night, you have to pay much attention to your newly-wedded instead of snoring off like a confirmed drunk. You may rather find dad making breakfast for Mum."

As we entered the house, I saw Mawumi was kind of right. Dad was not actually making breakfast but he was brewing coffee. He did not look quite hung over either.

"Hi Dad," I said. "I am surprised you are already up. I thought I would find you in bed groaning from a throbbing hangover."

"That is where I got you," he said. "Old chaps like us always prepare for such days. Before Viagra was created to help old men, another wise chap had developed some other stuff that could keep you sober enough after a serious drinking bout. I simply prepared myself, and here I am prepared to enjoy my morning coffee despite all the booze I took yesterday. I am sure if you go knocking on the doors of those friends who insisted on bringing me home yesterday, you will find all of them groaning with painful headaches."

"Unless they were as smart as you," I said.

"So, son," Dad said. "Have you come to raid my collection of gifts that my guests at the wedding so lavishly offered?"

"There is time for that, Dad," I said. "I have access to your store at any time."

"How did you enjoy my speech?" Dad asked.

"Where did you surface with all that crap, Dad?" I asked.

"You call that clever speech crap?" Dad asked. "You did not see the response from the guests? From the thunderous applause, every right-thinking man would conclude that I was in top form."

"I should admit that the response to your speech was very hectic, but I am sure it was because most marriages have been clogged with very dull speeches. For once, you came up with something the youth liked and the old men found kind of comic."

Just then Mum came out of the bedroom. She looked very much like a satisfied woman and smiled beautifully.

"I was making up the bed," She explained. "Your excited dad put much disorder there."

"And did not make up the bed himself?" I said. "You were not supposed to do any work today Mum. Dad was supposed to make up the bed, prepare breakfast, and do any other thing that looks like work."

"I am brewing coffee," Dad said. "Is that not enough work?"

"You simply went for the coffee to use it as a pick me up," I said. "You are brewing it for yourself not for Mum."

"Anyway," Dad said. "It is good that Mawumi has come. I am not really interested in you for now, but Mawumi could prepare a good breakfast for your mum and me."

"I did not bring my wife here to work," I said.

"Then, go and prepare the breakfast yourself," Dad said, "if you even know how to boil or fry an egg."

Mawumi had already moved to the kitchen where Mum joined her. I looked for my own cup and went for Dad's coffee.

"Kola coffee," I said. "Dad, you do have taste."

"I thought blokes like you drink tea," Dad said, sipping his coffee. "Son, did you see that my idea of remarriage was great?"

"It was quite an idea, Dad," I replied.

"Did you realize how many old girls were still falling for me?" Dad said. "It only shows you how striking I was when I was your age."

"I rather noticed most of your old chums admiring Mum," I said. "She was so radiant. She looked like a young bride being forced to marry an old man."

"That smacks of jealousy, son," Dad said. "But why don't we beef up this coffee with cognac before the women come back?"

"Good idea, Dad," I said. "You have reasoned like my real dad."

"You know I always do," Dad said. "It is just that at times I have to slow down to allow you catch up."

I went to the drinks cupboard and brought out a bottle of cognac. "Let's use our coffee mugs so that we look like innocent coffee drinkers," Dad proposed. "The women may complain that it is too early to hit the bottle."

We emptied our coffee mugs and I poured in liberal doses of cognac, before taking the bottle back. Like two old conspirators, Dad and I were enjoying our cognac and enjoying the conversation when the women finally came out of the kitchen with the breakfast.

We asked to be served where we were sitting and our dutiful wives obliged.

Half way through the meal, Dad smiled at Mum and put down his fork.

"Dear," he said. "Now that Mawumi and Akoni are here we could discuss our honeymoon. Several heads think better."

"Honeymoon?" Mawumi asked.

"Yes, honeymoon," Dad said.

"What do you need a honeymoon for?" I asked.

"We just got married," Dad said.

"But you are an old couple that simply needs quiet enjoyment in their home and a few visits from time to time by a beloved son and his wife."

"Don't forget that you will grow old someday," my father said. "Our honeymoon has to be expensive and colourful."

'After all you spent on your marriage, do you still have much left?" I asked.

"I may not be Croesus but I am not a poor man," Dad said. "Besides, my friends are paying for the honeymoon."

"You are one lucky old man," I said.

"When you are a good man, everything good comes your way," Dad said.

"So," Mawumi said, "where do you and Mum plan to go for this honeymoon?"

"We need ideas," Dad said. "That is why we are involving you in making a decision."

"Why don't you go to Bangkok?" I asked.

"Who told you we were looking for sex?" Dad replied.

"You could invite a lady boy and both you and mum could have fun with him," I said.

"Son, don't forget that you are talking to your mother and father," Mum said.

"Go to North Korea then if you rather need austerity," I proposed.

"No way," Dad said. "I won't take my wife to a place like that."

"They have spectacular military displays," I said. "Quite entertaining."

"But not to our taste," Dad replied.

"What of Greenland then?" I asked. "You two could go to Reykjavik."

"And stay indoors throughout because of the cold?" Mum asked. "Think of something better." "A good honeymoon requires lots of time indoors with the young bride," I said.

"Have you forgotten that I am your mother and not a young bride?" Mum asked. "If I am going on a honeymoon with your dad, it is for sightseeing and lots of fun, not a dreary bedroom."

"I propose Mexico. then," I said. "Lots of violence and boisterous scenes, lots of drugs and gang wars, and crowded beaches like in Cancun where you could admire young and old girls in bikinis and young lads in tight swimming trunks."

"If you don't have anything good to propose, better keep quiet," Dad said. "I suppose you would start advising us to go to Afghanistan and Iraq. There are so many good destinations, and you can't even think of one?"

"It depends on the kind of fun you want to have," Mawumi said. "We need to know whether you simply want to go shopping, visit historic museums, admire animals in the wild, or visit far off places."

"All of that I think," Dad said.

"I propose Tasmania then," Mawumi said.

"Why?" Dad asked.

"Tasmania is a far off place somewhere below Australia," Mawumi said. "There you can see marsupials, including the vicious Tasmanian devil."

"That is not much," Dad said. "In South Africa, we could visit kraals and parks teeming with all the dangerous animals. We could even visit the Island where Mandela was incarcerated for decades."

"I don't want South Africa," Mum said.

"What of the Pacific Islands of Fiji, Tonga, and Tahiti where you could eat breadfruit and roast pork?" I asked.

"I don't want a honeymoon with tears," Mum said.

"Let's take Japan then," I said.

"And get surprised by another tsunami?" Dad said.

"You two are making things very difficult," I said.

"It is rather you who is avoiding the right places and only hitting on the wrong ones," Dad said.

"Simply go to Britain, France, Germany, or America then," I said.

"And see what there that we have not seen before?" Dad asked. "This is a honeymoon, not an ordinary trip."

"There are these cruises around the world or to specific destinations by pleasure boats or cruise ships," Mawumi said. "Since you people cannot settle on any one place, go on a cruise."

"That could be it," Mum said.

"I am also inclined to think that Mawumi has brought out just what we needed."

"That calls for a drink, Dad," I said.

"We shall have lots of drinks on the ship," Dad said.

"We?" I asked. "Ah, yes! You and Mum."

"You are coming with us, son."

"Me?" I asked, stupefied.

"You and Mawumi," Dad said.

"Dad," I said, "that would no longer be a honeymoon. A honeymoon is meant for the two lovers to go out and enjoy themselves thoroughly."

"You are right, my son, and for your Mum and I, enjoying ourselves thoroughly means dragging you two along with us."

"It does not make sense," I said.

"But it does," Dad replied calmly. "Your mother is not a very good drinking partner. I make very good company, but there will be times when she will prefer good female company, especially when she cannot join me for a drink. Don't you see that this cruise will not be quite enjoyable without you?"

"Your Dad is right," Mum said. "The trip will be more exciting if I always have Mawumi to turn to for company when your dad decides to join the boys."

"Dad you know that Mawumi and I work hard to earn our daily bread. We are not retired, idle persons like you," I said.

"Mawumi has just applied for leave and I could work yours out with your boss." Dad said. "Do you want me to pay you for the pleasure of accompanying me on the trip?"

"Not pay. I can't take a salary from you. However, I won't mind receiving an ample amount as pocket money during the trip. I am still your son and deserve pocket money from you."

"That is still like a salary," Dad said. "Anyway, I can't rope you in to brighten up my honeymoon without enabling you to buy nice things for Mawumi at our various ports of call."

"Thank you, Dad," Mawumi said. "The trip will also enable us to see the world a little. And our trip will be a lot more comfortable than that of this chap in this book by Jules Vern. I think it is entitled 'Round the World in eighty days'."

Two days later I called Dad.

"When do we embark on this trip?" I asked.

"As soon as possible," Dad said. "I will see your boss first thing tomorrow. I suppose all your passports are in order. Fortunately, I came across an advert for one of these trips over the web. All we need to do is book, and in three days we shall take a plane to London where the cruise starts."

The next few days were quite busy as we prepared for our honeymoon trip.

We finally took off for Britain to catch the ship. When we landed at Heathrow airport, Dad turned to me.

"Son, you see how we both enjoyed ourselves together during the flight, especially with the booze, while your mum and Mawumi had enough time to exchange gossip. It could not have been that much exciting if only your Mum and I were closeted inside that plane.'

"It is true, Dad," I said. "Watching them conversing in that plane, one would have really concluded that they were mother and daughter, not mother and daughter-in-law."

"You see that at all cost I had to bring you along," Dad said.

"This means that if I had a real price or salary for the trip, I could push it up," I said.

"You are already well paid for this pleasure trip," Dad said. He had given me two thousand dollars as pocket money for the trip. "Besides, you have lots of free expensive booze along the line and all the feeding. I should instead ask you to return some of the money I gave you."

"I am your son and your pride," I said.

"With the women settled, we will go to the shipping company and confirm our trip."

"How do we get to Dunkirk?" I asked. "By boat train or bus?"

"I am sure it will be by boat train," Dad said.

Finally we were in the boat. We abandoned Vasco da Gama's and Magellan's sea route to India and opted for the Suez route. Since we were going round the world, we could not stop everywhere. Only very prominent places had been programmed for stop-over because of their tourist importance and strategic locations. On board the ship, there was every facility that could make the trip quite pleasurable. There were games, swimming pools, night clubs and bars, you name them. The meals were excellent and the ship attendants were quite polite and attentive.

There were a few naughty fellows on board though, who could have marred this wonderful trip if they had been given the chance, but the ship attendants were quite experienced and knew what to do in every case. There was one stout fellow who regularly got drunk and each time thought he was in a boxing ring and every other person around was the opponent. There was a lady who smiled enticingly at every attractive male, openly soliciting. There was this Nigerian pastor who kept trying to convert every potential donor to become a member of his church.

The couple in the next cabin to mine was on honeymoon too. They were not that young but they spent most of their time in their cabin.

"Don't you miss all the fun outside?" I asked the man when he joined Dad and me for a drink one day.

"There is more fun inside," He replied. "My wife wants it quite often, and I enjoy giving it to her. I prepared well for this before coming on the trip."

"You see the real honeymoon?" I asked Dad when the guy left us and rushed for another bout with his newly wedded.

"That is no longer fun," Dad said. "Some people do exaggerate."

"Maybe it is because he has the force," I said. "If you had that capacity, and an equally resistant and willing woman, wouldn't you give up all the other pleasures of the world?"

Dad had turned to his drink.

The biggest distraction came when an African tycoon from Niger, a huge, ugly fellow, declared that his *Grigri* had been stolen. There was much consternation among the passengers when he declared spiritual war and possible physical violence on whoever was the culprit. Many of the passengers had no idea what a *Grigri* was, but everybody got scared when the huge fellow started conducting a witch-hunting exercise. The ship attendants and ship security guards watched him closely. It turned out in the end that a female that he had taken from the nightclub to his cabin for the night had sneaked off with the stuff, convinced that it could be a very valuable museum artefact. She had concluded that she could sell it for millions if she succeeded in carting it off.

Our life on board followed a certain pattern. After breakfast in the morning, Dad and I played tennis or went swimming. After lunch and a short nap, we went for booze. On hot days, we had chilled beer. We had stronger stuff when it was cold. At times we simply relaxed on deck chairs, chatting away.

When not engaged in a game of scrabble or monopoly, or just women's talk, Mum and Mawumi often joined us for a drink. We went to night clubs a few times and watched a few spectacles from a few performers on board.

Whenever the ship stopped and we could disembark, we went ashore and strolled a bit but did not go far from the quay.

Life on the ship was interesting. While many of us were simply bent on enjoying our trip, there were some eccentrics who kept amusing us without realizing it.

There was this Corsican whose wife seemed to be attracted to every male on the ship. At each turn, the Corsican would threaten to cut open the stomach of whoever had caught her eye, just to end up crying pitifully and begging her to stick to him.

There was this lesbian couple where the husband was so pretty that one of the single men on the ship started struggling to transform her into a wife. This caused considerable misery to her wife, who could not imagine her loving husband taken away from her by a macho man.

A retired sumo wrestler was enjoying his honeymoon. His wife was a smallish Chukchi from Yakutia whom he had met and fallen for when he had gone to Russia as a tourist. She was so small beside him that you could hardly imagine them as husband and wife.

A handsome Swedish blonde, who had recently broken up with her long-time boyfriend, was using this pleasure trip to forget about him. She smiled freely at every prospective replacement, hoping to make a good catch.

There were two government ministers from some impoverished African countries squandering aid money meant for poverty alleviation. They had a new girl every day in their expensive cabins, drank champagne lavishly, and stood drinks around freely everywhere they happened to drink. Although they were inexperienced gamblers, they patronized the casinos and were very popular with all the gamblers. I later on learnt that they had come on board with female servants who doubled as concubines for whenever they did not succeed in getting a woman for siesta or for the night.

The nattily dresses Reverend Okafor did not miss having fun whenever he could. He argued that God made man in his own image and God was a jovial being who enjoyed good things. He had a following who gave freely to him because they understood that a true man of God must live well and have access to the best. He openly condemned another Nigerian pastor on board, Reverend Nwachukwu, for moving all over the place with a Bible in his hand, and always dressed as if his wardrobe was full only of second-hand clothes.

He insisted that his followers came to him on their own and supported him well. A good pastor did not have to go pleading with people to follow him.

We finally rounded up our trip and flew back home.

7

One week later, Dad came into my office, looking very excited. "Son," he said, "I have just had a swell idea. We are going to be rich."

"You are not badly off already," I replied. "Anyway, what is this swell idea that is expected to open the flood gates of this huge cash deposit?"

"I intend to go into consultancy," Dad said.

"But you are supposed to be retired from active duty and should be enjoying a well-deserved rest," I said. "Why would you want to give this up and go slaving for more money?"

"You don't understand, son," he replied. "I am not going to work for anybody. I will run my own consultancy and charge very high fees."

"Who is prepared to pay high fees for your ideas?" I asked. "I have never known you to be a best-seller when it comes to ideas and advice."

"That is where you know very little about your old man," he said. "I don't have big brains for nothing. You should be lucky that I was generous enough to pass some of it on to you or you would never have been this wonderful as a marketing expert."

"I take it back, Dad," I said. "How do you propose to make this fabulous fortune?"

"Let's start with my clients," he said. "They are all very rich, or at least well-to-do."

"How did you identify them?" I asked, interested

"They are all around," Dad said. "I am talking about my friends and acquaintances."

"And how do you propose to coerce them into becoming clients to your scheme?" I asked.

"It is quite easy, son," Dad said. "You remember the reception party when I was getting married again to your mother?"

"Who could forget it?" I said. "It was quite hectic. The groom's speech, the food, and most of all the booze."

"Forget about those," Dad said. "I am talking more about the guests. If you were keen enough to notice anything else apart from the drinks and beautiful women, you would have realized that half the hall was occupied by rich old fellows who have a lot more than they deserve or need."

"And what has that got to do with your consultancy?" I asked.

"Open your eyes, son," Dad said impatiently. "At times I wonder whether you are that clever. These rich old blokes are either married or are widowers. What has actually stirred me into recognizing the fact that I am a genius and a top expert in remarriage issues is the many calls I have already received. Many of them also want to remarry and would need expert advice on how to do it properly. From some of the calls, I could guess that they would even want me to prepare their speech for the occasion.

"That is wonderful, Dad" I said.

"Son, I am not dealing with poor entrepreneurs and struggling young chaps who are expecting to make it and need expert advice from a consultant. I am rather dealing with a crowd that has money and are prepared to dish it out to a resourceful consultant like myself on the least provocation."

"Some of these rich old men stick to their wallets as if their whole lives depended on it," I told Dad.

"Maybe," he said. "But if rub the right way the wallets generally spring open. Besides, many old men may be tight-fisted but when they need anything for themselves urgently, they pay for it."

"You are an old man and you know the eccentricities of your peers better than I," I said.

"You will get to be my age someday and will realize that life is sweetest at this age, especially when you can do your own things instead of relying on sons to do them."

"Hey, Dad," I said. "Don't take it badly. Well, if you prefer, I will rather call you a young man."

"That is even worse," Dad said. "It is rather old women who feel flattered when you mention that they look young even though they are actually aware of their real age."

"Okay, Dad," I said. "You want to become a consultant, open a big office full of pretty young secretaries, and advertise all over the place?'

"Don't make it look as if I am opening a brothel," Dad said. "Why would I need a bevy of pretty secretaries?"

"To attract your elderly clientele, of course," I said. "Most old fellows get excited in the midst of pretty young girls and that is when they become generous. If you have pretty secretaries, your elderly friends will keep coming to consult even if they have nothing to consult about."

"And what will your mother say if she came to the office and found me surrounded by pretty faces?" Dad asked. "She would think I opened the office for a different purpose."

"Anyway, Dad," I said, "you don't need an office. You could simply receive your clients in your study at home. After all, all you need to do is to give them advice."

"It won't look impressive at home," Dad said. "A consultant must present an aura around him that gives the client the impression that he is sitting in front of a superman. That is what makes him fall for any cheap advice you give."

"Okay, Dad," I said. "But you can't run an office alone. You could take Mum as your secretary and pay me to pop around once in a while as the technical adviser."

"I am supposed to be a consultant and give advice," Dad said. "What can a young chap like you contribute? And then, your mum is of a certain class and won't know how to play the role of a secretary. She may end up scaring away my clients."

"Now that you have rejected my mother and me, you can go ahead with your project alone."

"I thought you just said I cannot run an office alone," Dad said. "What I need you to do right now is to find me a good apartment that I can use as an office. Then recruit two smart girls, one as a secretary and the other for errands and other things."

"Where do you want this office of yours to be located?" I asked.

"Not far from here." Dad said. "I may have to call you for a drink now and again."

"Or to help you out when you get stuck with some difficult work," I said.

"What are you insinuating?" Dad asked. "Are you saying I won't be able to do all my consultancy work without help?"

I avoided the question.

"You know, you have just hired me to get you a good office and hire personnel,' I said. "That will cost you a pretty penny."

"Who said anything about paying?" Dad asked. "You should be thankful that your dad can still make millions and does not need to scrounge on you."

"Thanks, Dad, for the consideration," I said. "But I still need quite a sum of money for the rents, the installations, the furniture, and the equipment. Or do you want to sit in the lap of the secretary or have her sit on your lap? Even then, you will still need a chair for the one who is carrying the other."

"I will give you enough money," Dad said. "Just make sure that I have a good office and that the employees are quite smart."

For two weeks, I was torn between my own work and getting Dad's office ready. When everything was in place, I dived into the job market and rescued two pretty girls from the uncertainties of unemployment. Dad's office was now complete and work could start. If I had known that I would end up doing most of the odd jobs, I would have discouraged him from such a venture. I had to follow up and get the business registered, follow up the aspect of advertisements, especially in the Anlahsi club, and arrange for just every other thing including office supplies and drinks.

Dad's first day in office was nothing to write home about. No client turned up and after reading all the newspapers and watching TV, he sent the girls home and came interfering with my work.

"Dad," I protested "if you are idle, go home to your wife. I am at work and should pay attention to my work now, not to you."

"It is not closing time yet," Dad said. "You realize that I should not form the habit of shirking work and escaping home early."

"Then," I said, "go back to your office and keep waiting for clients. One might turn up."

"I would have done just that," he said, "but I needed a drink, and I can't drink without company."

"Can't you look for somebody else?" I asked. "I am busy."

"You should be happy that I consider you my best drinking partner," Dad said.

I succumbed, and regretted it later. For the next two weeks, Dad had no clients and kept insisting on giving me the pleasure of drinking with him. After all, he was paying.

Mercifully for me, by the end of two weeks Dad's customers started flowing in and Dad became so busy that I could concentrate fully on my work.

One day, however, I became quite curious as to what was transpiring in Dad's office and could not resist going across to peek and find out for myself. As I went into the outer office, one of my recruits, serving as receptionist, smiled at me very sweetly.

"Are you coming for business or pleasure?" she asked.

"What?" I asked in surprise.

"You appear too young to be a client here, but I need to know your reason for coming," she said.

"I recruited you," I said. "Remember?"

"Ah, it is you, sir," she said, recognizing me at last.

"So," I said. "What actually goes on here?"

"Nothing much, sir," she said. "Mr. Ngongnuwi programs and arranges remarriages for his elderly clients."

"Is that all?" I asked "I thought you equally asked me if I was coming for pleasure."

"Ah, that," she said. "Many of the old men come regularly and simply sit drinking with Mr. Ngongnuwi and require that we keep serving them. You need to see the way they keep ogling at us. One even attempted to pat my buttocks the other day."

"You let the dirty fellow do it?" I asked.

"No, sir. Mr. Ngongnuwi keeps warning them to use only their eyes and nothing else. He even tells them that, if one of them wants to make a pass at us, he should do it in a decent way."

"And they pay him money for simply sitting and ogling at pretty secretaries?" I asked, but realized that you cannot always understand what an old man will lavish money on, especially when it gives him much pleasure.

"Don't tell Dad that I was here," I said.

"You are not going to go in?" she asked.

"No," I said, leaving.

I would have to accost Dad and get an explanation. But then I needed to accost him alone.

That weekend, Mawumi and I went over to visit Mum and Dad. I hoped to take advantage of the visit and get things clear on the aspect of horny old men ogling at Dad's secretaries and even attempting to pat their rear ends. The idea was that Mawumi and Mum would have lots of gossip to exchange and would both get busy in the kitchen, thus giving me enough time alone with Dad to discuss at length. When we got there, however, Mum had a cold and Dad was busy proving his love for her by sitting next to her, frequently adjusting her muffler and handing her fresh Kleenex to use for her leaking nostrils. I immediately saw that my strategy had to be revised.

"Dad," I said after showing concern for mum's situation. "You must be tired already, having certainly served as a ministering angel all night and all day. Let Mawumi help you."

"I can never get tired of taking care of this sweetest lady in the whole wide world," Dad said bravely, earning a very lovely smile of gratitude from his wife.

"You need to rest a bit and continue after," I proposed. "While Mawumi and I are around, we should take over and let you have some rest. The rest of the day and the whole night are still there to give you the maximum opportunity of showing mum that you care."

"It is not about showing your mother that I care," Dad said. "I do care very much and she knows it."

"I understand, Dad," I said. "Let's have a drink on the veranda and discuss. There is some office work I want you to advise me on."

"You want to consult me for free?" Dad asked. "You should rather come to my office and pay for my services. Anyway, I am concerned with my wife now and have to stick by her."

"Mawumi is here to keep me company," Mum said. "Go and help your son."

"Will you be fine, dear?" Dad asked, concerned

"Quite fine," Mum said. "Besides Mawumi and I always have our things to discuss away from male ears."

"Make sure she is fine," Dad said to Mawumi..

I went to one of the cupboards and brought out a bottle of cognac, then I collected two glasses and went out to join Dad on the veranda.

"Dad," I said as we sat down.

"Yes, son," he replied. "What did you want to consult me about? I will do it for free this time, but next time, prepare your fee."

"I was just trying to get you away from the women so that we talk out of their hearing," I said. "What problem do you think I could have such that I would come for consulting?"

"Who knows," Dad said. "Anyway, what do you want us to discuss?"

"Dad,"' I said. "What actually goes on in your office?"

"What a stupid question!" Dad said. "It is a consultancy firm, people come and I help them with their remarriage programs."

"Is that all you do there?" I asked.

"What else do you think I do?" he asked.

"I noticed the high rate at which you replenish the drinks in your office. Do your clients drink that much?"

"You have been closely monitoring my purchases?" Dad asked. "Anyway, my friends have discovered that it is the best place away from home where they can relax, chat freely, and have a drink or two in good company without their wives interfering."

"Who pays for the drinks?" I asked.

"They do, of course," Dad replied. "It is part of the consultancy."

"And what is the role of the pretty secretaries in all this" I asked.

"The secretaries serve the drinks and snacks, and run out to buy more if there is any shortage," Dad said.

"I hope there is no molestation," I said. "Where ever you find dirty old men together with pretty young girls, there is bound to be some degree of stretching beyond bounds."

"My friends are not that dirty," Dad said. "It is normal for old men to be excited in the company of cute girls, but my friends have their limits."

"Even after several doses of good cognac?" I asked.

"I have cautioned them seriously against taking certain liberties. They simply enjoy the girls company, enjoy being served by them, and whatever happens further does not involve the office."

"What could happen further?" I asked.

"You never know," Dad said. "Some of these old men are quite smart and have a way of enticing young girls. So long as it is not quite open and does not disturb work, I have no objection to the girls consenting."

"I hope you are not that smart yourself, Dad," I asked.

"What do you mean?" he asked.

"You know, you being in the same office with these girls every day and you being their boss, and also an old man at that, you may not be dirty but you could be tempted."

"Watch out what you say young man," Dad said. "I may have faltered once with Miss Jam but that does not make me a lecher."

"One of the girls may fall for you and lure you into an affair," I said. "I hope they always dress well to work, no extra short skirts or blouses that expose too much of their breasts."

"You are the one who recruited them," Dad said. If they turn one to be bad, you should be blamed. However, so far they seem to be aware of the fact that they are working in a decent office and must maintain certain standards."

"Well, how is the consultancy coming?" I asked.

"Not bad," Dad said. "It keeps me busy, and I end up a few bucks richer every week."

"Keep it up, Dad," I said. "Maybe you will soon get included in the world record of millionaires who keep their money to maintain their position, deceive the world that they are in charity by donating a tiny fraction of their wealth, and keep making and amassing more wealth."

"I couldn't be like that," Dad said. "I have not told you yet, but I have already identified a few orphanages I will assist. And, as the consultancy grows, I will be doing much in health and education. I learnt a lot already from Newu's Foundation. I have planned to contribute to charity through that foundation, too."

"You will become some kind of Robin Hood?" I asked.

"What has simply handing over money that I don't need got to do with Robin Hood? My pension and income from certain investments are enough for me to live well. I simply intend to use this consultancy firm to keep active, and it would be stupid if I added the income from it to the money that I already have, so I simply intend to give it out to charity."

"You don't realize that what you are doing is the same as taking excess cash from your elderly clients and transferring it to charity?" I asked. "That is virtually what Robin Hood did. He robbed the idle rich and gave the money to the hard working poor."

"I get what you mean," Dad said. "I suppose it is something like that, although in my case the rich are not giving out of constraint."

"What you intend to do is a quite noble act, Dad." I said. "And I should learn from you. No need piling money in a bank account when the man next door cannot even have a decent meal a day. Maybe you should just transform this whole thing into a charity and fuse it with Miss Newu's Foundation."